Through the Valley

What God Says When the Shadow Is Real

Paul Hainline

To Mark and Bonnie.

You are not walking into the valley; you are walking through it.

The Shepherd is already there.

Through the Valley: What God Says When the Shadow Is Real

Published by NobleMind Press

ISBN 979-8-9954288-7-9

Printed in the United States of America

Contents

How to Use This Book

How to Use This Book

This book was not written to offer an explanation for the valley. It was written to provide a Companion within it.

Because the shadow is disorienting and the silence of God can feel like absence, these chapters are built on five specific principles meant to keep your feet on solid ground:

The Bible as Sole Authority. We do not rely on human tradition, near-death stories, or clinical speculation. Every word in these chapters is anchored in what the text actually says. When man says one thing and God says another, we believe God.

Word-for-Word Accuracy. We use the New American Standard Bible for its precision in rendering the original Greek and Hebrew. When a word in the original language adds genuine depth, we look at it closely. When it does not, we leave it alone.

Scripture Interprets Scripture. Where one passage is difficult, we look to the rest of the Bible to provide light. We let the revealed things sustain us while we leave the secret things to God (Deuteronomy 29:29). When the text is clear, we are clear. When the text is silent, we are silent.

Intellectual Honesty. This book will not offer platitudes. It acknowledges that the pain is real, the body decays, and the questions are often loud. It does not pretend the valley is not dark. It simply trusts that the Light is brighter.

A Shared Journey. These chapters are meant to be read together — by the one who is facing what is ahead and the one who is facing what will be left behind. The promises that sustain the one who is departing are the same promises that hold the one who remains.

A Note on "Through"

David did not say, "If I walk into the valley." He said, "Even though I walk *through*."

The valley is a passage, not a permanent home. It has an entrance and an exit. As you read, remember that the Third Strand — the God who has been woven into your lives from the beginning — is the One holding the cord together right now. He was there before the valley. He is here inside it. And He will be there when you walk out the other side.

This book is short enough to read in a hospital room. It is meant to be.

CHAPTER ONE

Even Though I Walk

"Even though I walk through the valley of the shadow
of death,
I fear no evil, for You are with me;"
— Psalm 23:4 (NASB)

You didn't choose this.

Nobody sits down one morning and decides that today is the day their life will divide into "before" and "after." Nobody plans for the conversation where a doctor's careful language lands in the room like a stone dropped into still water, and everything ripples outward from that moment. You didn't choose the diagnosis. You didn't choose the treatments that work for a while and then stop working. You didn't choose the hospital stays that grow longer and the stretches of home that grow shorter. You didn't choose any of this.

But here you are.

And if you are reading these words, you are probably in the hardest season a human being can walk through — the slow, grinding, day-by-day reality of watching someone you love move toward the end of their life on this earth. Or you are the one whose body is failing, watching your own strength leave you in measures that are sometimes sudden and sometimes so gradual you barely notice until you try to do something you did easily a month ago and find that you cannot. Either way, you know something that most people around you do not fully understand: this valley is real, it is dark, and it does not care about your schedule or your prayers or your plans.

This chapter is not going to fix that. Nothing written on a page can stop what is happening in your body or in your home. These words will not reverse a diagnosis or add months or take away the ache that settles in at two in the morning when the house is quiet and the future feels unbearable. If someone has handed you this book and told you it will make everything better, they meant well, but they promised you something no book can deliver.

What this chapter can do — what this whole book will try to do — is walk with you. Not around the valley. Not over it. Through it. And the first step of walking through something honestly is admitting where you are.

You Are in the Valley

David, the shepherd-king who wrote the twenty-third Psalm, did not say, "If I walk through the valley." He said, "*Even though* I walk through the valley of the shadow of death." The language assumes the valley is real and that the walk through it is happening. David was not writing about a hypothetical. He was writing about a certainty — one that every person who has ever drawn breath will eventually face, either for themselves or for someone they love.

But notice what David called it. He did not call it the valley of death. He called it the valley of the *shadow* of death. A shadow can be dark. A shadow can be frightening. But a shadow cannot actually harm you. A shadow requires a light source somewhere behind it — and the greater the light, the more defined the shadow becomes. The very fact that the shadow is so dark tells you that the light behind it is very bright.

That does not make the valley easier to walk through. Shadows are disorienting. They make it difficult to see where you are going. They play tricks on your perception and make threats feel closer than they are. And when you have been in the shadow for weeks or months, when the days blur together and the hospital room becomes more familiar than your own kitchen, it can feel like the shadow is all there is.

It is not. But you may not be able to see past it right now, and that is all right. David did not say, "I see the end of the valley." He said, "You are with me." The comfort was not in seeing the destination. The comfort was in the Companion.

The God Who Does Not Look Away

One of the cruelest lies that suffering whispers is that God has turned His face. That the silence in the room is the silence of heaven. That if He truly cared, if He truly had the power everyone says He has, then this would not be happening.

Scripture never makes that argument. What Scripture does, with remarkable honesty, is the opposite: it shows God walking *into* the suffering, not away from it.

Consider what happened at the tomb of Lazarus. Jesus had received word that His friend was sick. He stayed where He was for two more days. By the time He arrived, Lazarus had been dead for four days. Martha met Him on the road and said what anyone in her place would say: "Lord, if You had been here, my brother would not have died" (John 11:21). Mary came and said the same thing, word for word (v. 32). The people standing around were saying it too: "Could not this man, who opened the eyes of the blind man, have kept this man also from dying?" (v. 37).

And then comes one of the most important verses in the entire Bible:

> *"Jesus wept."*
> — John 11:35

Two words in English. One word in the Greek: *edakrusen* — He shed tears. Not metaphorical tears. Not a theological expression of sympathy. Real tears, from real eyes, running down a real face. And here is what makes this moment so staggering: Jesus *knew what He was about to do.* He was standing minutes away from calling Lazarus out of that tomb. He was not weeping because the situation was hopeless. He was weeping because the people He loved were in pain, and their pain moved Him — even though He held the power to reverse it.

That matters for you right now. It matters because it tells you something about the character of the God you are trusting with the hardest thing you have ever faced: He does not observe your suffering from a distance. He is not unmoved by it. He does not look at your tears and say, "They should be stronger than this." He looks at your tears and weeps with you. Even when He sees the whole picture that you cannot see. Even when He knows things about eternity that would change everything if you could know them too.

The writer of Hebrews tells us that we do not have a High Priest who cannot sympathize with our weaknesses, but One who has been tempted in all things as we are (Hebrews 4:15). The God who sits on the throne of the universe has been here. He has worn human skin, drawn human breath, felt human exhaustion, and wept real human tears at the grave of a friend. When you cry out to Him from the valley, you are not crying out to Someone who has to imagine what you feel. You are crying out to Someone who knows.

The Permission to Grieve

Somewhere along the way, a well-meaning tradition crept into the church that says strong faith does not grieve deeply. That if you really trust God, you will face loss with a steady voice and dry eyes and an unwavering confidence that everything is fine because heaven is real. That grief, especially prolonged grief, signals a deficiency of belief.

That is not what Scripture teaches.

When Jacob was told that Joseph was dead, he "tore his clothes, and put sackcloth on his loins and mourned for his son many days" (Genesis 37:34). Many days. Not an afternoon. When

David learned that Saul and Jonathan had fallen in battle, he composed a lament and ordered that it be taught to the people of Judah (2 Samuel 1:17–18). He institutionalized his grief. He made it public and permanent. When Job lost everything — his children, his livelihood, his health — he sat in ashes for seven days, and his friends sat with him in silence (Job 2:13). Seven days of saying nothing, because the grief was too heavy for words.

And then there is Paul, who wrote the single most important passage in the New Testament about Christian grief:

> *"But we do not want you to be uninformed, brethren, about those who are*
> *asleep, so that you will not grieve as do the rest who have no hope."*
> — 1 Thessalonians 4:13

Read that verse carefully, because it does not say what many people think it says. Paul did not write, *"so that you will not grieve."* He wrote, "so that you will not grieve *as do the rest who have no hope."* The distinction matters enormously. Paul assumed they would grieve. He expected it. Grief is the natural, God-given response of a heart that loves deeply when it faces separation. What Paul wanted them to understand was that their grief was not the same as the grief of those who have no hope. Not because it hurt less. Not because it was shorter. Not because faith gives you a shortcut through the valley. But because their grief carried something inside it that the world's grief does not: a promise.

We will come to that promise later in this book, and we will examine it closely, because you deserve to see exactly what God has said and not one word more or less. But for now, in this first chapter, the point is simpler and more immediate: *you are allowed to grieve.*

You are allowed to be exhausted. You are allowed to cry until you cannot cry anymore and then cry again the next morning. You are allowed to feel angry at the unfairness of it, confused by the silence of God, and afraid of what is coming. You are allowed to sit beside a hospital bed and hold a hand and have absolutely no idea what to say. You are allowed to drive home afterward and pull over because your eyes are too blurred to see the road. You are allowed to be a believer who is falling apart.

Because David was. Because Job was. Because Martha and Mary were. Because Jesus Himself stood at a graveside and wept. If grief were a failure of faith, then the Son of God failed at the tomb of Lazarus. And since that is not possible, grief must be something else entirely — something human, something holy, something that God Himself has made room for in the story He is writing.

The Shadow Is Not the Story

There is a detail in Psalm 23:4 that is easy to miss because the verse is so familiar that we tend to hear it as a single, undivided thought. But David actually said two things, and the second one matters as much as the first:

> *"Even though I walk through the valley of the shadow of death,*
> *I fear no evil, for You are with me;*
> *Your rod and Your staff, they comfort me."*
>
> — Psalm 23:4

The rod and the staff were the tools of a shepherd. The rod was used for protection — to fight off predators, to defend the sheep from danger. The staff, with its crook, was used for guidance — to pull a sheep back from a ledge, to direct it along the right path, to draw it close. David's comfort in the valley came not only from the shepherd's presence but from the shepherd's *activity*. God was not merely walking alongside him as a silent companion. He was actively protecting and actively guiding.

You may not be able to feel that right now. When you are deep in the valley, the rod and the staff are not always visible. The protection does not always look like what you asked for — you asked for healing, and what you have received is endurance. You asked for more time, and what you have received is the grace to be present in the time you have. That is not the answer you wanted. But it may be the rod and the staff doing exactly what they were designed to do: not removing you from the valley, but getting you through it.

And there is one more word in David's sentence that must not be overlooked: *through*. "Even though I walk *through* the valley." Not into. Not around. Through. The valley has an entrance, and the valley has an exit. It is a passage, not a permanent address. For the one who walks with the Shepherd, the shadow is not the final chapter. It is the hardest chapter. But it is not the last one.

This is where faith and grief walk side by side. They are not enemies. They are not contradictions. They are two responses to the same reality: that life in this world involves loss, and that the God who made this world has not left us alone in it. You can hold both at the same time — the grief that says *this is devastating* and the faith that says *He is with me*. Neither one cancels the other. Neither one needs to wait its turn.

A Word to Both of You

If you are walking this valley together — one of you facing what is ahead, the other facing what will be left behind — then you already know something that no one outside your door fully understands: you are grieving the same loss from two completely different directions.

One of you is coming to terms with leaving. The other is coming to terms with remaining. One of you watches your body weaken and wonders what the transition will feel like. The other lies awake at night in a house that already feels too quiet and wonders what the first morning alone will be like. You are in the same valley, but you are not having the same experience of it, and there are days when the distance between those two experiences feels almost as painful as the valley itself.

This book is written for both of you. Not in separate sections — his chapter and her chapter, the dying and the living. That kind of division would only widen the distance that the valley is already trying to create between you. Instead, every chapter in this book is meant to be read by both, because the promises of God that sustain the one who is departing are the same promises that sustain the one who remains. The Shepherd walks with both of you. The rod and the staff protect and guide both of you. The valley has an exit for both of you — though you will not walk out of it at the same time, and that is one of the hardest truths in this entire book.

But you are not alone in it. Not either of you. And you are not alone with each other, which is something, but you are also not alone with just each other. There is a third Presence in the valley, and He has been there longer than you have.

> *"The LORD is near to the brokenhearted*
> *and saves those who are crushed in spirit."*
> — Psalm 34:18

Not near to the strong. Not near to those who have it all figured out. Near to the brokenhearted. Near to the crushed. If that is where you are today, then by God's own word, you are exactly where His presence is closest.

The valley is real. The shadow is real. The grief is real. And so is He.

That is where we begin.

Reflection Questions

1. David said, "You are with me." In what specific moment this week have you sensed — or struggled to sense — God's presence in the valley?

2. This chapter says grief and faith are not enemies. Where in your own experience have you tried to choose one over the other instead of holding both?

3. "The shadow is not the story." What shadow feels most overwhelming right now, and what would it look like to trust the light behind it?

CHAPTER TWO

For You Are With Me

"Do not fear, for I am with you;
do not anxiously look about you, for I am your God.
I will strengthen you, surely I will help you,
surely I will uphold you with My righteous right
hand."

— Isaiah 41:10 (NASB)

There are moments in this valley when God feels very far away.

You know the moments. They come at two in the morning when you cannot sleep and the house is so quiet that you can hear the clock on the wall and nothing else. They come in the hospital room when the machines are humming their steady, indifferent rhythm and the person you love is sleeping and you are sitting in a chair that was not made for sitting in for hours, watching their chest rise and fall and wondering how many more times you will watch it. They come in the car on the way home when a song comes on the radio that belonged to a different season of your life, a season when the future was something you looked forward to instead of something you dreaded.

In those moments, the silence of God can feel enormous. You have prayed. You have begged. You have bargained, though you know bargaining is not how prayer works. You have asked for healing and received treatment plans. You have asked for a miracle and received another scan. You have poured out your heart to the Creator of the universe, and what has come back — or what seems to have come back — is silence.

If you have felt this, you are not the first believer to feel it, and you are not failing.

--- --- --- --- --- --- ---

Silence Is Not Absence

David knew this silence. The man who wrote "The LORD is my shepherd" also wrote this:

> *"How long, O LORD? Will You forget me forever?*
> *How long will You hide Your face from me?*
> *How long shall I take counsel in my soul,*
> *having sorrow in my heart all the day?"*
>
> — Psalm 13:1–2

That is not a man who had everything figured out. That is a man who loved God deeply and could not understand why God was not answering. "How long" appears four times in two verses. It is the language of someone who has been waiting and waiting and the waiting has become its own kind of suffering. David did not whisper this prayer politely. He cried it out. He accused God of forgetting him. He asked God how long His face would remain hidden.

And God put it in the Bible.

That matters. God did not edit David's frustration out of the record. He preserved it. He put it in the hymnal of His people, where it has been read and sung and prayed for three thousand years by believers who found themselves in the same silence and needed to know that they were not the first to wonder where God had gone. The very fact that Psalm 13 exists in Scripture is itself an act of comfort: God is not offended by your honesty. He is not threatened by your questions. He would rather you cry out to Him in confusion than retreat into a silence of your own.

But here is what David knew, even in the crying out, even in the "how long" — and what you can know too: silence is not the same thing as absence. A parent who is quiet in the next room has not left the house. A shepherd who does not speak is still watching. God's silence in your suffering does not mean He has removed Himself from your situation. It may mean that what He is doing cannot yet be explained in terms you would understand. It may mean that the answer He is giving does not sound like the answer you asked for. It may simply mean that His presence in this season is something you will have to trust before you can feel it.

And David, even from the depths of Psalm 13, arrived at exactly that trust. The same psalm that begins with "How long will You forget me?" ends with this:

> *"But I have trusted in Your lovingkindness;*
> *my heart shall rejoice in Your salvation.*
> *I will sing to the LORD,*
> *because He has dealt bountifully with me."*
>
> — Psalm 13:5–6

Nothing changed between verse 1 and verse 5. David's circumstances did not improve in the space of four verses. God did not suddenly appear with an explanation. What changed was that

David made a decision — not a feeling, a *decision* — to trust in the lovingkindness of a God who had not yet answered him. That is not blind faith. That is faith built on a history of faithfulness. David had seen God deliver him before. He had seen the rod and the staff at work in a hundred earlier valleys. And he chose, in the silence, to trust what he had already seen rather than doubt what he could not currently feel.

You may be in Psalm 13:1 right now. That is all right. But Psalm 13:5 is written by the same hand, in the same breath, about the same God. Hold on to it even if you cannot feel it yet.

Through the Waters, Through the Fire

God spoke through the prophet Isaiah to a people who had every reason to believe they had been abandoned. Israel was heading toward exile. Their world was coming apart. And into that coming darkness, God said something that was not a promise of rescue from the suffering but a promise of presence *within* it:

> *"But now, thus says the LORD, your Creator, O Jacob,*
> *and He who formed you, O Israel,*
> *'Do not fear, for I have redeemed you;*
> *I have called you by name; you are Mine!*
> *When you pass through the waters, I will be with you;*
> *and through the rivers, they will not overflow you.*
> *When you walk through the fire, you will not be scorched,*
> *nor will the flame burn you."*
> — Isaiah 43:1–2

Study the structure of that promise. God did not say "if" you pass through the waters. He said "*when*." He did not promise the waters would not come. He did not promise the fire would not burn. He promised that when they came — not if, when — He would be there. The waters would not overflow. The flame would not consume. Not because the danger was not real, but because the Presence in the danger was greater than the danger itself.

And before He said any of that, He said something that is easy to rush past but that carries the full weight of the passage: "I have called you by name; you are Mine." The promise of presence is rooted in the promise of possession. You belong to Him. Not in the abstract, not as a line item in a cosmic ledger, but by name. He knows your name. He knows the name of the one you love who is lying in that hospital bed. He knows both of you by name, and you are His, and the waters that are rising around you right now have not changed that and cannot change that.

There is a moment in the book of Daniel that brings Isaiah's promise out of poetry and into visible, historical reality. Three young men — Shadrach, Meshach, and Abed-nego — were thrown into a furnace for refusing to worship Nebuchadnezzar's image. The fire was heated seven times hotter than normal. The soldiers who threw them in were killed by the heat. And then Nebuchadnezzar looked into the furnace and said:

> *"Look! I see four men loosed and walking about in the midst of the fire without harm, and the appearance of the fourth is like a son of the gods!"*
> — Daniel 3:25

Three went in. Four were seen walking. The fourth figure appeared only *inside* the furnace. He was not standing outside shouting instructions. He was not watching from a safe distance. He was in the fire with them, walking where they walked, present in the very place where the heat was most intense.

That is the character of your God. He does not wait for you on the other side of the fire. He does not stand outside the valley and call to you to hurry through. He enters it. He walks in it. And His presence in it does not remove the heat, but it changes what the heat can do. The fire burned the ropes that bound them. It did not burn them. When they came out, the text says their clothes did not even smell like smoke (Daniel 3:27).

You are in a furnace right now. The heat is real. And the Fourth Figure is in it with you.

When the Answer Is Not What You Asked For

There is a prayer that Paul the apostle prayed that does not get enough attention in conversations about suffering. It is important here because it is the prayer of a faithful man who asked God to remove something painful and was told no:

We do not know what the thorn was. Paul did not say, and centuries of speculation have not produced a definitive answer. But we know several things about it: it was physical or deeply personal ("in the flesh"), it was painful enough that Paul called it torment, and Paul wanted it gone badly enough to plead with God three separate times.

God said no. But He did not simply say no and walk away. He said, "My grace is sufficient for you." In other words: I am not going to take this from you, but I am going to be in it with you, and what I give you in it will be enough. Not enough to make it painless. Not enough to make it make sense. Enough.

This is one of the hardest truths in all of Scripture, and it would be dishonest to soften it. Sometimes God's answer to our most desperate prayer is not the removal of the suffering but the provision of His presence and His grace within it. You have probably prayed for healing. You may still be praying for it, and you should — God hears prayer, and miracles are not impossible. But if healing does not come in the way you have asked for it, that does not mean God did not answer. It may mean that His answer is what He said to Paul: My grace is sufficient. My power shows up best in your weakness. I have not left you. I am enough.

Paul's response to God's answer reveals something remarkable about what happens when a person accepts the sufficiency of grace, even in the absence of the answer they wanted:

> *"Most gladly, therefore, I will rather boast about my weaknesses, so that the power of Christ may dwell in me. Therefore I am well content with weaknesses, with insults, with distresses, with persecutions, with difficulties, for Christ's sake; for when I am weak, then I am strong."*
> — 2 Corinthians 12:9–10

Paul did not say he enjoyed the thorn. He did not say he stopped wanting it removed. He said he found a strength in his weakness that he could not have found any other way. The thorn did not become pleasant. It became the place where the power of Christ was most visible.

Your valley may be that place. Not a punishment. Not an oversight. Not evidence of God's absence. But the place where, stripped of every self-sufficiency, you discover that He really is enough. That His grace really does hold. That the promise "I will be with you" really does mean something when every other comfort has been taken away and all that remains is Him.

He Is Here

Let us return to where this chapter began — to the quiet room, the late hour, the feeling that God is very far away.

He is not.

He is the God who preserved the cries of David in sacred Scripture so that you would know your own cries are not strange to Him. He is the God who said "when you pass through the waters" — not if — and promised to be in them with you. He is the Fourth Figure in the furnace, visible only when the fire is hottest. He is the One who said to Paul, "My grace is sufficient," and meant it — not as a dismissal of Paul's pain, but as a declaration of His own faithfulness.

He is the Shepherd whose rod protects and whose staff guides, even through the darkest valley. Even when you cannot see the rod. Even when you cannot feel the staff. Even when the shadow is so thick that you can barely see the next step in front of you.

David said, "I fear no evil, for You are with me." David did not say, "I fear no evil because I understand what is happening," or "because I can see the way out," or "because I feel Your presence." He said, "You are with me." The reason for his courage was not understanding or feeling. It was a fact. God was with him. Period. Whether he felt it or not. Whether the valley made sense or not. Whether the shadow lifted or lingered.

That same God is with you tonight. In the hospital room. In the quiet house. In the car when the tears come and you cannot stop them. In the conversation you do not know how to have. In the fear you have not spoken out loud to anyone.

He is not far away. He is not silent because He is indifferent. He is present — as present as He was in the furnace, as present as He was at the tomb of Lazarus, as present as He was when He said to Paul, "My grace is sufficient."

You may not feel Him. Trust the promise anyway. Feelings rise and fall. The word of God stands.

> *"The grass withers, the flower fades,*
> *but the word of our God stands forever."*
>
> — Isaiah 40:8

His word says He is with you. He is with you.
32

Reflection Questions

1. David moved from "How long will You forget me?" to "I have trusted in Your lovingkindness" within the same psalm. What would your own psalm look like if you wrote it honestly today?

2. God's answer to Paul was "My grace is sufficient." Where in this valley have you received an answer that was not the one you asked for — and what has it looked like to live with it?

3. The Fourth Figure appeared only inside the furnace. Have you experienced a closeness to God that came specifically because of the fire, not in spite of it?

CHAPTER THREE

My Flesh and My Heart May Fail

"My flesh and my heart may fail,
but God is the strength of my heart and my portion
forever."
— Psalm 73:26 (NASB)

Your body used to do what you told it to.

There was a time — and it may not feel that long ago — when you got out of bed without thinking about it. When you walked to the kitchen and poured your own coffee and drove yourself wherever you needed to go. When your hands were steady and your legs were reliable and the basic mechanics of living were so automatic that they required no thought at all. Your body was a tool you used without noticing it, the way you use a light switch without thinking about the wiring behind the wall.

Now you notice everything. You notice the weight of a glass of water. You notice the distance from the bed to the bathroom. You notice the effort it takes to form a sentence on a day when the medication is heavy or the exhaustion has settled in so deeply that even your words feel slow. You have become a student of your own decline, tracking losses that no one else sees — the things you could do last month that you cannot do this month, the capabilities that slip away so quietly that sometimes you only discover they are gone when you reach for them and find nothing there.

This chapter is for you. Not for the person sitting beside your bed, though they may read it too. This is for the one whose body is betraying them. The one who is still fully present inside a frame that is shutting down around them. The one who knows what is happening and has to live inside that knowledge every waking hour.

What Scripture says to you in this place is not what you might expect. It does not minimize what you are losing. It does not tell you to pretend the decline is not real. It says something far more extraordinary than that.

The Outer Man and the Inner Man

Paul knew something about physical suffering. His body bore the scars of a ministry that most of us can barely imagine. He had been beaten with rods three times, received thirty-nine lashes five times, been stoned and left for dead, been shipwrecked three times, and spent a night and a day adrift in the sea (2 Corinthians 11:24–27). He carried a thorn in the flesh that God refused to remove, and he labored under conditions that would have broken most people long before they broke him.

This was not a man writing about suffering from a comfortable distance. This was a man whose body had been systematically dismantled by the demands of his calling. And from that body, with those scars, he wrote something that may be the most important passage in the New Testament for the person whose flesh is failing:

"Therefore we do not lose heart, but though our outer man is decaying, yet our inner man is being renewed day by day. For momentary, light affliction is producing for us an eternal weight of glory far beyond all comparison, while we look not at the things which are seen, but at the things which are not seen; for the things which are seen are temporal, but the things which are not seen are eternal."

— 2 Corinthians 4:16–18

Read that first sentence again: "Though our outer man is decaying, yet our inner man is being renewed day by day." Paul did not deny the decay. He named it plainly. The outer man — the body, the physical frame, the part of you that the doctors are treating and the cancer is attacking — is decaying. Paul used the present tense. It is happening. It is ongoing. He did not pretend otherwise.

But he set it against something else that is also happening, also ongoing, also in the present tense: the inner man is being renewed. Day by day. Not *despite* the decay, but *concurrent with* it. Two things are happening to you at the same time. One of them is visible to everyone who walks into your room. The other is visible only to God and, in quiet moments, to you. Your body is failing. And something inside you that is not your body is being made new.

You may have experienced this already without having a name for it. There are moments, even in the worst of this — maybe especially in the worst of this — when something clarifies. When the things that used to matter so much simply fall away, and what remains is a kind of clear-eyed vision of what was always real: God, the people you love, the faith that has carried you this far, the hope of what comes next. The outer man loses things every day. But the inner man, stripped of everything unnecessary, sometimes sees more clearly than it ever did when the body was strong and the world was full of distractions.

Paul called the suffering "momentary" and "light." That may sound almost offensive to someone who has been enduring months of treatment and pain and hospital stays. But Paul was not measuring the suffering against a human timeline. He was measuring it against eternity. Against the weight of glory that the suffering is producing. And in that comparison — the only comparison that ultimately matters — even the longest suffering is brief, and even the heaviest suffering is light. Not because it feels light. Because of what it is being weighed against.

--- --- --- --- --- --- --- ---

The Tent and the Building

Paul did not stop at verse 18. He continued directly into one of the most vivid images in all his writing:

> *"For we know that if the earthly tent which is our house is torn*
> *down, we have a building from God, a house not made with*
> *hands,*
> *eternal in the heavens."*
>
> — 2 Corinthians 5:1

The image is unmistakable. Your body is a tent. Tents are temporary by nature. They are useful, even necessary, but nobody confuses a tent with a permanent home. A tent wears out. Its canvas thins. Its poles weaken. Its seams eventually fail. That is not a defect in the tent. That is what tents do. They were never built to last forever.

But when the tent comes down, there is a building waiting. Not another tent. A building. A house not made with hands. Eternal. In the heavens. Paul chose his words with precision. Everything about the tent is temporary, fragile, earthly, handmade. Everything about the building is permanent, solid, heavenly, God-made. The contrast is total.

What you are experiencing right now is the tent wearing out. The canvas is thinning. The seams are giving way. And it is hard — harder than anyone who has not been through it can understand — because you are still living inside the tent while it comes apart around you. You are aware of every new tear, every weakening pole, every part of the structure that used to hold and no longer does.

But you are not the tent. That is the point Paul is making, and it is the point this chapter exists to deliver to you. Your body is something you inhabit. It is not something you are. The *you* who thinks, believes, loves, prays, remembers, and hopes — that person is not decaying. That person is being renewed day by day. And that person has a building from God waiting — not a wish, not a theory, but a certainty that Paul stated in the indicative: "we *have* a building from God." Present tense. It already exists. It is already yours.

Paul went even further:

> *"For indeed in this house we groan, longing to be clothed with our dwelling from heaven, inasmuch as we, having put it on, will not be found naked. For indeed while we are in this tent, we groan, being burdened, because we do not want to be unclothed but to be clothed, so that what is mortal will be swallowed up by life."*
>
> — 2 Corinthians 5:2–4

The groaning is real. Paul did not dismiss it or spiritualize it away. He said *we groan* — including himself. But the groaning is not the groan of despair. It is the groan of anticipation. It is the discomfort of a caterpillar in the chrysalis, not the misery of a creature without hope. Something is coming. What is mortal will be swallowed up — not by death, but by life. The mortality does not win. The life wins. The tent falls, and what replaces it is not emptiness but something so substantial that mortality itself is consumed by it.

The Indignity of Dependence

There is an aspect of this season that Scripture does not address directly in a single proof text but that runs beneath the surface of many passages, and it must be spoken to honestly: the loss of independence.

You may have reached the point where you need help with things you have done for yourself your entire adult life. Getting dressed. Getting to the bathroom. Eating. You may need someone to manage your medication, help you move from the bed to the chair, drive you where you need to go. You may have gone from being the person in your family who did things for others to being the person others do things for, and that shift carries its own quiet grief that has nothing to do with dying and everything to do with dignity.

If you feel that grief, you are not being proud. You are being human. God made you to work, to act, to contribute. From the beginning, He gave Adam a job before He gave him a wife (Genesis 2:15). The ability to do things — to provide, to help, to carry your own weight — is woven into what it means to bear the image of God. Losing that ability, piece by piece, is a real loss. It is not vanity to mourn it.

But here is what you need to hear, and what the people around you may not know how to say: your value in the eyes of God has never been a function of what you can do. It has always been a function of whose you are.

Consider the last week of Jesus' life on this earth. The Son of God, who had healed the sick, calmed the sea, fed thousands, and raised the dead, spent His final hours in a condition of complete physical helplessness. He was arrested. He was bound. He was struck in the face by men who were not worthy to speak His name. He was nailed to a cross where He could not move His hands or His feet, could barely draw breath, and had to push up against the nails just to fill His lungs enough to speak. He was dependent on a stranger to carry His cross. He was dependent on a soldier to offer Him something to drink. He was, in every physical sense, utterly powerless.

And He was, in that very moment, accomplishing the most important work in the history of the universe.

His value did not decrease when His body was broken. His identity did not diminish when He could no longer stand under His own power. The cross was not the failure of His mission. It was the fulfillment of it. And the most powerful act God has ever performed in human history was carried out by a Man who could not even wipe the blood from His own eyes.

You are not useless because you are dependent. You are not less because you need help. The kingdom of God has never measured worth the way the world measures it. The world measures by output, productivity, self-sufficiency. God measures by faithfulness, trust, and the willingness to let Him be your strength when yours is gone.

> *"But He said to me, 'My grace is sufficient for you, for power*
> *is perfected in weakness.'"*
>
> — 2 Corinthians 12:9a

Power is perfected in weakness. Not *despite* weakness. *In* it. The weakness is not the obstacle to God's work. It is the location of it.

What the Mirror Cannot Show You

There is a version of you that the mirror shows and a version of you that the mirror cannot show. The mirror shows the tent. It shows the thinning canvas, the weakening frame, the effects of treatment and disease and the slow accumulation of days in the valley. The mirror tells a story of decline, and that story is not false — but it is incomplete.

The version of you that the mirror cannot show is the one that Paul described as being "renewed day by day." It is the version that has been bought with the blood of Christ (1 Corinthians 6:19–20), sealed with the Holy Spirit (Ephesians 1:13–14), and held in the hand of a God from which no one and nothing can snatch you (John 10:28–29). It is the version that is known by name by the Creator of the universe, loved before the foundation of the world, and destined for an inheritance that is imperishable, undefiled, and will not fade away (1 Peter 1:4).

The tent is failing. But the person inside the tent is being held by hands that do not fail.

Asaph, the psalmist who wrote Psalm 73, arrived at this truth from a place of deep frustration. He had watched the wicked prosper while he suffered, and he nearly lost his faith over it. He said his feet had almost slipped (Psalm 73:2). He envied the arrogant (v. 3). He saw their ease and it made his own pain feel unbearable and unjust. But then he entered the sanctuary of God, and everything shifted:

> *"Whom have I in heaven but You?*
> *And besides You, I desire nothing on earth.*
> *My flesh and my heart may fail,*
> *but God is the strength of my heart and my portion forever."*
> — Psalm 73:25–26

My flesh and my heart may fail. Asaph did not say "if." He said "may" — as in, even when it happens, even when it is happening right now. The flesh fails. The heart fails. But God does not fail. And God is not merely a helper in the crisis. He is the *portion.* The inheritance. The thing itself. When every other possession has been stripped away, when the body can no longer function, when the heart can no longer pump on its own, God remains. And He is enough. Not enough in addition to other things. Enough by Himself. The strength of the failing heart. The portion that does not diminish.

Forever.

You Are Still Here

This chapter has spoken hard truths. The body is a tent. Tents come down. The outer man decays. These are not comfortable things to read when the decay is happening to *your* body, in *your* room, on *your* watch.

But here is the truth that holds all the other truths together: you are still here. Right now, today, you are alive. Your eyes are reading these words. Your mind is turning them over. Your spirit is reaching toward the God who has not let go of you and will not let go of you. Whatever today holds, it holds you in it, and God holds today.

You do not know how many days remain. Neither does the person who loves you most and is reading this beside you or in the next room. But every one of those days is a day in which the inner man is being renewed. Every one of those days is a day in which the eternal weight of glory is being produced. Every one of those days is a day in which God is the strength of your heart and your portion.

The tent is temporary. You are not.

And what is coming — what is already yours, already built, already waiting — is not a tent. It is a building from God. A house not made with hands. Eternal in the heavens.

Hold on. The canvas is thin. But what is on the other side of it is more solid than anything you have ever known.

Reflection Questions

1. Paul described the body as a tent and what awaits as a building. When you look at the physical decline — yours or your loved one's — how does this distinction change how you process it?

2. This chapter speaks about the "indignity of dependence." If that is where you are, what has been the hardest thing to let go of — and what, if anything, has become clearer because of it?

3. "My flesh and my heart may fail, but God is the strength of my heart and my portion forever." What does it mean for God to be your portion when everything else is being stripped away?

CHAPTER FOUR

Two Are Better Than One

*"Two are better than one because they have a good
return for their
labor. For if either of them falls, the one will lift up his
companion.
But woe to the one who falls when there is not another
to lift him up."*

— Ecclesiastes 4:9–10 (NASB)

You are losing him in pieces.

Not all at once. Not in a single moment that you can point to and say, "That is when everything changed." It has been slower than that, and in some ways the slowness is the cruelest part. A little less energy this week than last. A medication that stops working, replaced by another that works differently, or less. A conversation that he would have carried easily six months ago but that now exhausts him in minutes. An afternoon where he sleeps and you sit beside him with nothing to do but watch and wait and try not to think too far ahead.

You are grieving, and he is still here. That is one of the most disorienting experiences a human being can have. The world has a word for the person whose spouse has died. It does not have a good word for the person whose spouse is dying. You occupy a space that has no name — no longer the wife whose husband is healthy, not yet the woman who has lost him, but something in between that carries the weight of both without the resolution of either.

If anyone has told you that you should not be grieving yet — that you should be "staying positive" or "being strong for him" or "focusing on the time you have left" — they mean well, but they do not understand what you are carrying. You are not grieving prematurely. You are grieving *accurately.* The loss is already happening. It is happening every day, in small withdrawals that add up to something enormous, and your heart knows it even when your words cannot explain it.

This chapter is for you.

--- --- --- --- ---

Naomi Knew

There is a woman in Scripture who understood the kind of loss that hollows you out from the inside. Her name was Naomi, and the book of Ruth tells her story with a honesty that has no equal in ancient literature.

Naomi and her husband Elimelech left Bethlehem during a famine and settled in the land of Moab. There, both of their sons married Moabite women. And then, in the space of what the text covers in three verses, everything came apart: Elimelech died. Then both sons died. Three sentences in the Hebrew text. An entire life dismantled.

When Naomi decided to return to Bethlehem, she told her daughters-in-law to go back to their own families. Ruth refused. She clung to Naomi with words that have been read at weddings for centuries, though they were not spoken by a bride to a groom but by a bereaved woman to another bereaved woman: "Where you go, I will go, and where you lodge, I will lodge. Your people shall be my people, and your God, my God" (Ruth 1:16).

But it is Naomi's words, not Ruth's, that matter most for this chapter. When they arrived in Bethlehem and the women of the town recognized her and called her by name, Naomi said:

> *"Do not call me Naomi; call me Mara, for the Almighty has dealt*
> *very bitterly with me. I went out full, but the LORD has brought*
> *me back empty."*
>
> — Ruth 1:20–21a

Naomi means "pleasant." Mara means "bitter." She was not being melodramatic. She was being devastatingly honest. She had left this town with a husband and two sons. She was returning with nothing but a Moabite daughter-in-law and a grief so deep that she could no longer bear to hear her own name. "I went out full, but the LORD has brought me back empty."

And God put those words in Scripture. He did not correct her. He did not insert an editorial note explaining that she should have been more grateful for what she still had. He did not send a prophet to tell her that her attitude was unbecoming of a woman of faith. He let her speak her emptiness, and He recorded it as sacred text, because the emptiness was real and God does not require His people to perform contentment they do not feel.

You may know this emptiness. You may know what it means to feel it settling into your bones while the person you love is still breathing in the next room. The house already feels different. The future already feels hollow. The chair he used to sit in, the side of the bed he used to sleep on, the particular way he said your name — you are already beginning to memorize these things with a new kind of attention, the attention of someone who knows they are cataloging what will soon become memories.

That is not weakness. That is love doing what love does when it faces separation. And if Naomi could stand in the gate of Bethlehem and rename herself after her bitterness and still be held by God, carried by God, and ultimately redeemed by God — then you can be honest about yours.

— — — — — — — —

The Exhaustion No One Sees

There is a particular kind of tiredness that belongs to the person who is caring for someone who is dying, and it is different from any other kind of tiredness in the world.

It is not the tiredness of a long day at work, which a good night's sleep can fix. It is not the tiredness of a difficult week, which a weekend can restore. It is a tiredness that goes to the center of who you are and sits there, and sleep does not fully reach it, because even when your body rests your mind does not. You lie in bed and listen for sounds from the other room. You check your phone to see if the hospital has called. You run through medication schedules and appointment dates and insurance questions and the dozen decisions that nobody warned you would fall on your shoulders, and you do all of this while carrying a grief that has no outlet because the person you would normally talk to about your hardest days is the person you are grieving.

That last part deserves to be said again. For most of your life, when things were hard, you talked to him. He was your sounding board. Your processing partner. The person who sat across from you at the kitchen table and listened while you worked through whatever was weighing on you. And now the heaviest thing you have ever carried is the losing of him, and you cannot take it to him without adding to the weight he is already carrying himself. So you hold it. You hold it in the car. You hold it in the shower. You hold it at three in the morning when there is no one to tell and no one to hear and the loneliness is so thick you can almost touch it.

The psalmist wrote:

> *"I am weary with my sighing;*
> *every night I make my bed swim,*
> *I dissolve my couch with my tears.*
> *My eye has wasted away with grief."*
> — Psalm 6:6–7a

That is not poetic exaggeration. If you have spent nights soaking your pillow with tears you did not choose and could not stop, David has been where you are. And David was not a weak man. David was a warrior, a king, a man after God's own heart. And he dissolved his couch with his tears. The Bible does not present this as failure. It presents it as the reality of a human heart under unbearable pressure. Your exhaustion is not a sign that you are doing this wrong. It is a sign that you are carrying something enormously heavy and you have been carrying it for a long time.

There is a promise in Scripture that speaks directly to this kind of bone-deep weariness:

> *"Do you not know? Have you not heard?*
> *The Everlasting God, the LORD, the Creator of the ends of the earth*
> *does not become weary or tired.*
> *His understanding is inscrutable.*
> *He gives strength to the weary,*
> *and to him who lacks might He increases power.*
> *Though youths grow weary and tired,*
> *and vigorous young men stumble badly,*
> *yet those who wait for the LORD*
> *will gain new strength;*
> *they will mount up with wings like eagles,*
> *they will run and not get tired,*
> *they will walk and not become weary."*
>
> — Isaiah 40:28–31

Notice the progression. Eagles. Running. Walking. Most people read this passage and focus on the soaring. But Isaiah ordered it deliberately. Sometimes you soar. Sometimes you run. And sometimes — in seasons like this one — the victory is simply walking and not becoming weary. Putting one foot in front of the other. Getting through the day. Making it to the hospital and back. Holding his hand for another hour. Walking, not growing weary.

That is not failure. That is Isaiah's third promise, and it is no less miraculous than the first. The strength to walk without growing weary when everything in you wants to collapse — that is God's strength. Not yours. His. Given to the weary. Increased for the one who lacks might.

You lack might right now. That is not a confession of weakness. That is the qualification for the promise.

When Fighting Becomes Holding

There may come a day — and it may have already come — when the thing you have always done for him no longer helps him.

You have spent years, perhaps decades, being the one who pushes. The one who encourages him to get up, to try again, to not give in. That is what partners do. That is what love does. It believes the best, hopes for more, refuses to quit. And for most of your life together, that push was exactly what he needed.

But there is a kind of pushing that becomes a weight instead of a lift. And when his body begins to say *I cannot,* your encouragement — however lovingly meant — can start to feel like disappointment. Like expectation he cannot meet. Like one more way he is failing you, even though failing you is the last thing he wants to do.

This is not your fault. You are doing what you have always done. You are loving him the way you have always loved him. The problem is not your love. The problem is that the rules have changed, and no one told you when they changed or what the new ones are.

Here is what you need to hear: *letting him rest is not the same as letting him go.*

There is a difference between giving up and surrendering. Giving up is what happens when hope dies. Surrendering is what happens when someone stops fighting *against* and begins resting *in*. Jesus did not give up in the garden of Gethsemane. He surrendered. "My Father, if it is possible, let this cup pass from Me; yet not as I will, but as You will" (Matthew 26:39). He was not defeated. He was yielded. And the yielding was not weakness — it was the deepest act of trust a human being has ever performed.

Your husband's body may be telling him something his words cannot say yet. He may not have the language for it. He may not even fully understand it himself. But somewhere inside him, a shift may be happening — a turning from the fight to keep the tent standing toward a readiness for what comes after the tent. And if that is where he is, then your job is not to pull him back. Your job is to walk with him there.

This does not mean you stop caring. It does not mean you stop offering. It means you hold your offerings with an open hand instead of a closed one. You say, "Would you like to try to eat something?" instead of "You need to eat." You say, "I'm here if you want to try to stand" instead of "You have to keep working at this." You give him permission to say no without feeling like he has failed you.

The writer of Ecclesiastes said:

> *"There is an appointed time for everything. And there is a time for every event under heaven... a time to search and a time to give up as lost; a time to keep and a time to throw away."*
> — Ecclesiastes 3:1, 6

There is a time to fight. And there is a time to stop fighting — not because hope is gone, but because the nature of the hope has changed. The hope is no longer that the body will recover. The hope is what it has always been underneath: that the Shepherd is leading, that the valley has an exit, that what is waiting on the other side is very much better.

If he is ready to stop fighting the disease and start resting in the promise, then the most loving thing you can do is not to drag him back into a battle his body has already decided it cannot win. The most loving thing you can do is sit beside him. Hold his hand. Stop pushing and start simply being present.

You are not giving up on him. You are giving him permission to go where he is going — at his pace, in his time, with you beside him instead of pulling against him.

And the guilt you feel — the voice that says *a good wife would make him fight harder* — that voice is lying to you. A good wife loves her husband. You are loving him. The shape of that love is changing because the shape of what he needs is changing. That is not failure. That is faithfulness.

Let him rest. Stay beside him. And trust that the Shepherd who has been leading both of you through this valley knows exactly when it is time to stop walking and when it is time to lie down in green pastures.

He will not leave either of you. Not now. Not ever.

The Guilt That Has No Right to Be There

There is something else you are carrying that you may not have spoken aloud to anyone, and it needs to be named so it can be set down.

You have thought about "after."

Not in a planning, practical way — although there is that, too, and it carries its own burden. But in the deeper way. You have caught yourself, in an unguarded moment, imagining the house without him. Imagining a morning when you wake up and he is simply not there and will not be there again. Imagining what holidays will feel like, what Sundays will feel like, what the silence will sound like when it is no longer the silence of someone sleeping in the other room but the silence of genuine absence.

And then the guilt arrived. Because how dare you think about that while he is still alive. How dare your mind go to that place while he is still fighting, still here, still needing you to be present. It feels like betrayal. It feels like you are mentally burying him before his time. It feels like a failure of love, a failure of faith, a failure of the kind of devotion that a wife is supposed to have.

It is none of those things.

Your mind is doing what minds do when they face an approaching reality: it is trying to prepare. It is trying to build some small framework, however fragile, for what is coming, because human beings are not designed to face enormous loss with no preparation whatsoever. The fact that your thoughts go to "after" does not mean you have given up on "now." It means you are a human being who is facing the hardest thing she has ever faced, and your mind is reaching ahead, trying to find ground that will hold.

Jesus Himself anticipated the cross before He reached it. In the Garden of Gethsemane, He was not yet on the cross, but His soul was already in the suffering:

> *"Then He said to them, 'My soul is deeply grieved, to the point of*
> *death; remain here and keep watch with Me.' And He went a*
> *little*
>
> *beyond them, and fell on His face and prayed, saying, 'My Father,*
> *if it is possible, let this cup pass from Me; yet not as I will,*
> *but as You will.'"*
>
> — Matthew 26:38–39

Jesus grieved the thing before it happened. He felt the weight of it before it landed. His soul was grieved "to the point of death" — and the cross was still hours away. If the Son of God experienced anticipatory grief, then it is not a failure for you to experience it. It is human. It is the natural response of a heart that can see what is coming and cannot stop it.

Let the guilt go. It does not belong to you. You are not betraying him by thinking about the future. You are loving him in the present while being honest about what the present is leading toward. Those are not contradictions. They are the two hands of the same faithful heart.

— — — — — — — — —

You Were Not Meant to Carry This Alone

Solomon, the wisest man who ever lived apart from Christ, wrote the words that open this chapter:

— Ecclesiastes 4:9–12

You have lived the truth of this passage for years. You know what it means to have someone who lifts you when you fall, who keeps you warm when the world is cold, who stands with you when you would otherwise stand alone. That is what marriage is, and that is what makes the approaching loss so devastating: you are losing the person who was built into the structure of how you survive.

But notice where Solomon ended: "A cord of three strands is not quickly torn apart." Two strands are good. Three are stronger. And in a marriage built on faith, the third strand has always been God. He has been woven into your life together from the beginning — in the prayers you prayed side by side, in the Scriptures you studied together, in the faith that has held you both through every season that came before this one.

When one strand is taken away, the third strand does not unravel. It holds. It was always the strongest strand in the cord. It was the one that kept the other two from breaking in the storms that came before this one, and it will keep you from breaking in this one too. Not because the pain will be less. But because the God who has been woven into your marriage from the beginning will still be woven into your life after it.

The psalmist wrote:

"The LORD is near to the brokenhearted
and saves those who are crushed in spirit."

— Psalm 34:18

We read this verse in Chapter 1, and it returns here because it is more specific to your situation than it might appear at first glance. The Hebrew word for "near" is *qarov* — it means close, present, intimate. Not near in the sense of being in the same general area. Near in the sense of being right beside you. The LORD is *right beside* the brokenhearted. Not watching from across the room. Not monitoring from a distance. Right there. In the chair beside the bed. In the driver's seat on the way home. In the kitchen at midnight when the house is too quiet and the tears come again.

You were not meant to carry this alone. And you are not carrying it alone, even when it feels like you are. The Third Strand holds.

What You Are Doing Matters

Before this chapter closes, something needs to be said that you may not be hearing from anyone else, because the people around you may not know how to say it, or may not realize it needs to be said:

What you are doing right now is one of the most sacred things a human being can do.

You are being present with someone you love in their most vulnerable hours. You are showing up day after day to a situation that offers you nothing but heartbreak, and you are showing up anyway. You are managing medications and making decisions and absorbing information that no one should have to absorb, and you are doing it with a broken heart. You are sitting in hospital rooms when you would rather be anywhere else on earth, because the person in that bed matters more to you than your own comfort. You are, in the truest and most literal sense, laying down your life for another person — not in a single dramatic moment, but in the slow, unglamorous, day-after-day way that real love actually works.

Jesus said:

> *"Greater love has no one than this, that one lay down his life for his friends."*
> — John 15:13

You are doing that. Not on a battlefield. Not in front of an audience. In a hospital room, in a quiet house, in the thousand invisible decisions of a caregiver who has nothing left to give and gives anyway. That is greater love. And it does not go unseen by the God who watches sparrows fall and numbers the hairs on your head.

You may feel like you are not doing enough. You may feel like a better wife would be handling this with more composure, more faith, more grace. You may look at yourself and see only the cracks — the moments you lost patience, the nights you resented the exhaustion, the times you walked into the bathroom and closed the door and fell apart because you could not fall apart in front of him.

Those are not failures. Those are the fracture lines of a heart that is carrying more than it was designed to carry. And the God who is near to the brokenhearted is not cataloging your fractures. He is holding you together through them.

"He heals the brokenhearted
and binds up their wounds."

— Psalm 147:3

He heals. He binds. Not after the valley is over. In it. Right now. In the binding, in the holding, in the quiet sustaining of a woman who gets up every morning and walks back into the hardest thing she has ever done because love will not let her stay away.

You are not failing. You are not falling apart. You are walking, and not fainting, and that is the eagle's promise dressed in ordinary clothes.

And you are not alone.

Reflection Questions

1. Naomi renamed herself Mara — "bitter" — and God recorded it without correction. What name would you give yourself in this season, and what does it tell you that God is not offended by your honesty?

2. Isaiah described a progression: eagles, running, walking. Which one describes where you are right now — and can you accept that walking without fainting is its own miracle?

3. "You are not alone." The Third Strand — God woven into your life — holds even when one strand is taken. Where have you seen evidence of that holding, even in small ways?

CHAPTER FIVE

What No Eye Has Seen

"Things which eye has not seen and ear has not heard,
and which have not entered the heart of man,
all that God has prepared for those who love Him."
— 1 Corinthians 2:9 (NASB)

At some point in this valley — late at night, or in a quiet moment between hospital visits, or in the car on the way home when the radio is off and there is nothing between you and your own thoughts — the question surfaces. It may come as a whisper or it may come with the force of a wave, but it comes:

What happens next?

It is the oldest question human beings have ever asked, and the one that every generation has tried to answer. Philosophers have speculated. Poets have imagined. Religions have constructed elaborate frameworks. Near-death accounts have been published by the thousands, each one claiming a glimpse behind the curtain. The world is flooded with voices telling you what happens after the last breath, and most of them are guessing.

This chapter is not going to guess. It is not going to speculate, and it is not going to build a picture from sources outside of Scripture. What it is going to do is walk carefully through what God has actually said. Not one word more. Not one word less. Because what He has said, though it does not answer every question you have, answers the ones that matter most — and answers them with a certainty that no human speculation can match.

--- --- --- --- ---

What Paul Knew

The apostle Paul faced death more times than most people can count. He was beaten, stoned, shipwrecked, imprisoned, and threatened by his own countrymen, by Gentiles, by false brothers, and by the Roman state. He wrote many of his letters from prison cells, fully aware that any of them might be his last. If anyone in the New Testament had reason to think carefully about what lay on the other side of death, it was Paul.

And he was remarkably clear about it. Writing to the church at Philippi from a Roman prison, not knowing whether he would live or die, Paul said:

> *"For to me, to live is Christ and to die is gain. But if I am to live on in the flesh, this will mean fruitful labor for me; and I do not know which to choose. But I am hard-pressed from both directions, having the desire to depart and be with Christ, for that is very much better; yet to remain on in the flesh is more necessary for your sake."*
>
> — Philippians 1:21–24

Read that slowly, because Paul was not speaking in the abstract. He was facing the real possibility of execution, and he was telling the Philippians what he actually felt about it. And what he felt was *torn*. Not between living and annihilation. Not between existence and emptiness. He was torn between two *good* things: fruitful labor here and being with Christ there. He wanted to stay because the people he loved still needed him. He wanted to go because what was waiting for him was, in his own words, "very much better."

The Greek phrase Paul used — *pollō mallon kreisson* — is emphatic. It is not "a little better" or "somewhat better." It is "far better," "very much better," "better by far." Paul stacked comparatives. He wanted there to be no ambiguity about what he was saying: to depart and be with Christ is not merely acceptable, not merely a relief from suffering, not merely the end of pain. It is *very much better* than the best this life has to offer. And Paul's life, for all its suffering, was not a small life. He had seen churches planted across the Roman Empire, lives transformed by the gospel, and the resurrected Christ Himself on the road to Damascus. Yet all of that, weighed against what was waiting for him, was the lesser thing.

Notice also what Paul assumed about the timing. He did not say, "I desire to depart and eventually, at some future date, after a period of unconscious waiting, be with Christ." He said, "to depart and be with Christ." The departure and the being with Christ are presented as immediate. One follows the other without a gap. For the believer, death is not a passage into uncertainty. It is a passage into presence.

Absent from the Body, at Home with the Lord

Paul said the same thing even more directly in his second letter to the Corinthians. After the passage about the tent and the building that we explored in Chapter 3, he continued:

> *"Therefore, being always of good courage, and knowing that while we are at home in the body we are absent from the Lord — for we walk by faith, not by sight — we are of good courage, I say, and prefer rather to be absent from the body and to be at home with the Lord."*
>
> — 2 Corinthians 5:6–8

The language Paul chose here is the language of *home.* He did not say "to be absent from the body and to exist in some other state." He said "to be at home with the Lord." Home. The word carries everything you feel when you have been away for a long time and finally walk through your own door. The ease. The familiarity. The sense of being where you belong. Paul is saying that for the believer, death is not going *away* from home. It is going *to* home. The body was the temporary dwelling. The presence of the Lord is the permanent one.

And notice the word "courage." Paul used it twice in three verses: "being always of good courage" and "we are of good courage." This was not the language of a man who was nervous about what lay ahead. It was the language of a man who knew where he was going and was at peace with it. Not because he had all the details. Not because someone had drawn him a map of the afterlife. But because he knew *who* was there. The destination was not a place. It was a Person.

That matters enormously for the person who is facing death and wondering what the transition will feel like. Scripture does not give us a moment-by-moment description of the passage from this life to the next. It does not tell us what the first five seconds are like, or the first five minutes, or the first five hours. What it tells us is *who is on the other side.* And who is on the other side is the same Christ who walked on water, calmed the storm, raised the dead, and said, "I am the resurrection and the life; he who believes in Me will live even if he dies" (John 11:25). The details of the crossing are not revealed. But the One who meets you on the far shore is fully revealed, and He is not a stranger. He is the Savior who has known you and carried you your entire life.

What Jesus Himself Said

On the night before His crucifixion, Jesus gathered His disciples in an upper room and spoke to them about what was coming. He knew they were afraid. He knew they were confused. And He said:

> *"Do not let your heart be troubled; believe in God, believe also in Me. In My Father's house are many dwelling places; if it were not so, I would have told you; for I go to prepare a place for you. If I go and prepare a place for you, I will come again and receive you to Myself, that where I am, there you may be also."*
>
> — John 14:1–3

There are four things in these three verses that deserve careful attention.

First, Jesus began with a command that is also an invitation: "Do not let your heart be troubled." He did not say, "Do not be sad." He did not say, "Stop feeling what you feel." He said, "Do not let your heart be troubled." It is a call to a decision, not a denial of emotion. The trouble is real. The choice is whether to let it govern you or to set it against something bigger.

Second, He said, "In My Father's house are many dwelling places." The Greek word is *monai* — dwelling places, abiding rooms, permanent residences. Not temporary quarters. Not a waiting room. A home within the Father's house, prepared specifically for those who belong to Him. The imagery is of a household large enough for everyone, where no one is an afterthought and no one is crowded out.

Third — and this is one of the most tender things Jesus ever said — He added, "If it were not so, I would have told you." Think about what that means. Jesus was saying: I would not let you believe something that was not true. I would not allow you to walk toward a hope that does not exist. If the Father's house were not real, if the dwelling places were not there, if the promise were empty — I would have told you. I would not deceive you. Not about this. The fact that I am telling you this is itself the proof that it is true, because I do not lie to the people I love.

Fourth, He said, "I will come again and receive you to Myself, that where I am, there you may be also." The purpose of the destination is not the place. It is the presence. "That where *I am*, there *you* may be." The promise is not merely a better location. It is an unbroken, permanent, face-to-face companionship with Christ. Whatever heaven is in its details — and Scripture reveals some of those details, as we will see — the center of it, the reason it is home, is Him.

What Will Be Gone

Near the end of the Bible, in the final chapters of Revelation, God pulled the curtain back further than anywhere else in Scripture and allowed the apostle John to see what is coming:

> *"And He will wipe away every tear from their eyes; and there will no longer be any death; there will no longer be any mourning, or crying, or pain; the first things have passed away."*
> — Revelation 21:4

Read that verse against everything you are living through right now. Every tear. Every death. Every morning of mourning. Every hour of pain. Every night of crying. God did not say these things would be reduced or managed or made bearable. He said they would be *gone.* "The first things have passed away." Everything that belongs to this fallen, broken, cancer-ridden world — all of it — categorized by God as "first things" and declared passed away. Finished. Over. Not diminished. Eliminated.

And notice the intimacy of the first image: "He will wipe away every tear from their eyes." Not "tears will cease." Not "crying will stop." *He* will wipe them away. Personally. Individually. The Creator of the universe, with His own hand, wiping tears from the faces of His children. That is not the language of a distant deity managing a cosmic program. That is the language of a Father holding His child's face and gently wiping away every trace of sorrow.

For the one whose body is failing: there will be no more pain. No more nausea. No more exhaustion. No more needles, no more scans, no more waiting rooms, no more results. The body that has been your burden will be replaced with something that does not decay, does not ache, does not fail.

For the one who is watching and waiting: there will be no more grief. No more hospital drives. No more three-in-the-morning fear. No more holding together what keeps trying to fall apart. Every tear you have shed in this valley — every single one — will be wiped away by a hand that has known your face since before you were born.

———————

What Will Be There

Scripture does not give us a floor plan of heaven. It does not describe it in the kind of architectural detail that would satisfy our curiosity. And there is a reason for that. Paul hinted at it when he wrote to the Corinthians:

> *"Things which eye has not seen and ear has not heard,*
> *and which have not entered the heart of man,*
> *all that God has prepared for those who love Him."*
> — 1 Corinthians 2:9

The reason Scripture does not describe heaven in complete detail is not that God is withholding information to be mysterious. It is that the reality exceeds the capacity of human language to convey. What God has prepared has not entered the heart of man. Your best imagination, your most vivid dream, your most expansive conception of what "wonderful" means — none of it has reached what is actually there. It is not that the description would be disappointing. It is that the description is impossible. The thing itself is too large for the words.

But Scripture does tell us some things, and what it tells us is enough.

It tells us that Christ is there. "To depart and be with Christ" (Philippians 1:23). "Absent from the body, at home with the Lord" (2 Corinthians 5:8). "Where I am, there you may be also" (John 14:3). Whatever else heaven contains, it contains the presence of the One who loved you enough to die for you and who rose again so that death would not have the final word over your life.

It tells us that rest is there. "Blessed are the dead who die in the Lord from now on... so that they may rest from their labors" (Revelation 14:13). For the one who has been fighting a disease that will not relent, who has endured treatment after treatment, who has watched their own body become a battleground — there is rest. Real rest. Not the temporary relief of a good day between bad ones. Rest that does not end.

It tells us that wholeness is there. Paul wrote that the body is sown "in dishonor" but raised "in glory," sown "in weakness" but raised "in power," sown a natural body but raised a spiritual body (1 Corinthians 15:43–44). Whatever the resurrected body is, it is not the broken version you are living in now. It is the version God always intended — free from decay, free from limitation, free from the long humiliation of disease. The seed that goes into the ground does not look like the tree that comes up. But the tree was always inside the seed.

And it tells us that recognition is there. Paul wrote to the Thessalonians about the return of Christ and the gathering of believers, and his entire argument in 1 Thessalonians 4:13–18 assumes that the relationships we have in this life carry into the next. He told the Thessalonians to "comfort one another with these words" — and the comfort would mean nothing if the reunion were not a reunion of people who knew each other. The separation is real. But it is not permanent. The people you love in Christ, you will see again — and you will know them, and they will know you.

--- --- --- --- ---

The Thief on the Cross

There is one more passage that must be included in this chapter, because it addresses a fear that many people carry but rarely voice: the fear that at the moment of death, something could go wrong. That somehow, even after a life of faith, the passage itself might be uncertain or frightening or lonely.

On the cross, hanging beside Jesus, there were two criminals. One mocked Him. The other said:

> *"Jesus, remember me when You come in Your kingdom!"*
> — Luke 23:42

And Jesus replied:

> *"Truly I say to you, today you shall be with Me in Paradise."*
> — Luke 23:43

Today. Not eventually. Not after a waiting period. Not after a review of his record. Today. This man had no time to build a lifetime of service. He had no opportunity to prove himself or earn his way. All he had was a moment of faith and a dying Savior next to him. And Jesus said, "Today you will be with Me."

The thief's request was modest: "Remember me." He did not ask for Paradise. He asked to be remembered. And Jesus did not merely remember him. He brought him home.

The generosity of God's grace in that moment is almost too large to hold. A criminal, in his last hours, received the same promise that Paul the apostle spent a lifetime anticipating: to be with Christ. Today.

That promise holds for every believer. The transition from this life to the next, for the one who belongs to Christ, is not a leap into darkness. It is a step from the tent into the building. From the temporary into the permanent. From the shadow into the light. And the One who meets you on the other side is not a judge behind a bench. He is the Savior who hung on a cross beside a thief and said, "Today. With Me. In Paradise."

For Both of You

This chapter has spoken about what comes next primarily from the perspective of the one who is going. But it is written for both of you, because the promises in these pages sustain both sides of the valley.

If you are the one whose body is failing: what is ahead of you is not an ending. It is an arrival. Paul called it "very much better." Jesus called it "My Father's house." The writer of Revelation described it as a place where every tear has been wiped away and death itself has been destroyed. You are not walking toward darkness. You are walking toward the most real, most solid, most alive thing that exists. And the One who is preparing the place knows your name.

If you are the one who will remain: the same God who receives him receives you. The same promises that comfort him are meant to comfort you. The separation is real, and no one is asking you to pretend it is not. But the separation is temporary, and the reunion will be permanent. The day is coming when you will see him again, not weakened by disease, not diminished by treatment, but whole. Raised in glory. Raised in power. And you will know him, and he will know you, and the valley will be behind both of you forever.

Jesus said, "If it were not so, I would have told you."

He cannot deceive you. It is not in His nature. The God who spoke the universe into existence with words does not use those words carelessly, and He does not make promises He will not keep. The dwelling places are real. The reunion is real. The absence of pain, the absence of tears, the absence of death — all of it is as certain as the character of the God who promised it.

You do not know what eye has not seen. You cannot imagine what has not entered the heart of man. But you know who prepared it. And you know He said it was very much better.

That is enough.

Reflection Questions

1. Paul called the departure "very much better." If you are the one whose body is failing, does that phrase bring comfort or does it feel distant? If you are the one remaining, how does it land differently for you?

2. Jesus said, "If it were not so, I would have told you." What does it mean to you that the God who cannot lie has staked His character on this promise?

3. Revelation 21:4 says God will wipe away every tear personally. As you sit with the specific pain of this season — the scans, the exhaustion, the fear — what would it feel like for all of that to be gone?

CHAPTER SIX

Things Too Wonderful for Me

"I have declared that which I did not understand,
things too wonderful for me, which I did not know."
— Job 42:3 (NASB)

The question does not always come in words. Sometimes it is just a feeling — a weight behind the eyes at three in the morning, a tightness in the chest in the hospital parking lot, a silence in the middle of a prayer that was going fine until it wasn't. But when it does find words, it is always some version of the same question.

Why?

Why him? Why this? Why now? And the variation that cuts deepest of all: what did he do to deserve this?

He didn't. That needs to be said immediately and plainly, before another word is written. What is happening to Mark is not a punishment. It is not a consequence of hidden sin. It is not God settling an account. The Bible does not teach that every instance of suffering is traceable to a specific failure, and the one book in Scripture that most thoroughly addresses that idea — the book of Job — exists in large part to dismantle it.

But knowing that the suffering is not a punishment does not make the question go away. It only removes the wrong answer. The space where the right answer should be remains empty.

This chapter will not fill that space. Not because the question does not matter — it does. Not because God is offended by it — He is not. But because the Bible does not provide a specific answer to why this man, this disease, this timeline. And a book that claims to stand on Scripture cannot offer what Scripture does not give.

What this chapter will do is walk with you to the place where the question was asked more loudly than anywhere else in all of Scripture — and show you what God did with it.

The Man Who Asked

His name was Job. He was blameless and upright, one who feared God and turned away from evil. God Himself said so — twice (Job 1:8, 2:3). And in the space of a single day, he lost nearly everything. His livestock. His servants. His children — all ten of them. Then his health. He sat among the ashes and scraped his skin with a piece of broken pottery, and his wife told him to curse God and die (Job 2:9).

He did not curse God. But he did ask why.

He asked loudly. He asked repeatedly. He asked with a rawness that has made Bible readers uncomfortable for three thousand years. "Why did I not die at birth, come forth from the womb and expire?" (Job 3:11). "What is my strength, that I should wait? And what is my end, that I should endure?" (Job 6:11). He demanded an audience with the Almighty: "Oh that I had one to hear me! Behold, here is my signature; let the Almighty answer me!" (Job 31:35).

This was not a man whispering polite questions into a journal. This was a man in agony, shouting at the sky, demanding to know why the God he had served faithfully had allowed his life to be torn apart.

And here is what matters most: God did not rebuke Job for asking.

The Friends Who Had Answers

Before God spoke, Job's friends spoke. For thirty-five chapters. Eliphaz, Bildad, Zophar — and later Elihu. They arrived with theology, logic, and explanations. They had a framework, and they were determined to make Job's suffering fit inside it.

Their framework was simple: God blesses the righteous and punishes the wicked. You are suffering. Therefore you must have sinned. Repent, and He will restore you.

They said some true things along the way. They spoke accurately about God's power, His sovereignty, His holiness. Eliphaz was not wrong that God is greater than man (Job 33:12). Bildad was not wrong that God does not pervert justice (Job 8:3). The problem was not the individual pieces. The problem was the conclusion they built from them — that Job's suffering could be explained, categorized, and resolved with the right theological formula.

They were wrong. And God told them so directly.

This is one of the most important verses in the entire book, and it is easy to miss in the rush to get to the ending. The friends who tried to explain the suffering were rebuked. The man who sat in the ashes and cried out — who said things that were raw, unfiltered, and at times bordered on accusation — was the one God said had spoken rightly.

God does not rebuke honest grief. He rebukes tidy explanations that misrepresent Him.

This matters for you — for both of you — because you will encounter people who try to explain what is happening. People who mean well. People who love you. And some of them will say things like "God has a plan" or "everything happens for a reason" or "He must need another angel in heaven." They will say these things in waiting rooms and church hallways and text messages, and however kindly they are meant, they will land like stones on an open wound.

Job's friends were not bad people. They were wrong people. And the difference between the two matters enormously when you are the one sitting in the ashes.

You do not owe anyone an explanation for your grief. You do not owe anyone a performance of peace you do not feel. And when the well-meaning answers come — and they will — you are free to let them pass without carrying them. The God who rebuked the explainers is the same God who honored the man who simply told the truth about his pain.

When God Speaks

Job 38. After thirty-five chapters of human theology, God arrives. Out of the whirlwind. And He does not explain.

> *"Where were you when I laid the foundation of the earth?*
> *Tell Me, if you have understanding, who set its measurements?*
> *Since you know. Or who stretched the line on it?*
> *On what were its bases sunk? Or who laid its cornerstone,*
> *when the morning stars sang together*
> *and all the sons of God shouted for joy?"*
>
> — Job 38:4–7

Four chapters of questions. Not accusations — questions. The foundations of the earth. The boundaries of the sea. The storehouses of snow and hail. The constellations in their courses. The hawk that soars by God's wisdom. The war horse that laughs at fear. Behemoth. Leviathan. God walks Job through the created order — not to humiliate him, but to reorient him. To show him that the universe operates at a scale and a complexity that no human mind can hold.

Not one of these questions addresses Job's suffering directly. Not one explains why. God does not say "here is why I allowed this." He does not open the curtain on the conversation with Satan from chapters one and two. He does not offer a formula. He does not apologize.

He says, in effect, "Here is who I am."

And that turns out to be the answer — not the answer Job was looking for, but the answer Job needed. Because the question behind the question was never really "why is this happening?" The question behind the question was "can I trust the God who is allowing it?" And God's response — this breathtaking tour of His power, His wisdom, His intimate involvement in every corner of creation — was not a deflection. It was the most direct answer possible to the real question.

If this is the God who holds the sea in its boundaries and calls the stars by name and knows when the mountain goat gives birth on a cliff face no human eye has ever seen — then this is a God whose judgments can be trusted even when they cannot be understood.

What Job Found

Job's response, when it comes, is not what you might expect from a man who has spent thirty-five chapters demanding answers.

> *"I know that You can do all things, and that no purpose of Yours can be thwarted."*
>
> — Job 42:2

> *"I have declared that which I did not understand, things too wonderful for me,*
> *which I did not know."*
>
> — Job 42:3

That word — "wonderful." In Hebrew, *nipla'ot,* from the root *pala.* It does not mean pleasant or enjoyable. It means beyond human capacity to comprehend. Things that exceed the boundaries of what a finite mind can hold. The same root appears in Psalm 139:6 — "Such knowledge is too wonderful for me; it is too high, I cannot attain to it." And in Psalm 131:1, where David said, "I do not involve myself in great matters, or in things too wonderful for me."

Job was not saying his suffering made sense now. He was saying he had been speaking about things that operate at a level he could not reach — and he knew it now. The questions did not go away. They got repositioned. They moved from the center of his vision to the periphery. Not because they stopped mattering, but because something larger moved into the center.

> *"I have heard of You by the hearing of the ear; but now my eye sees You."*
>
> — Job 42:5

Before the valley, Job knew *about* God. Inside the valley, Job *knew* God. The secondhand became firsthand. The theology became encounter. Hearing became seeing.

This is the hardest truth in this chapter, and it must be said gently: sometimes the valley is where God becomes most real. Not because suffering is good — it is not. Not because God sends disease to teach lessons — that is the theology of Job's friends, and God rejected it. But because when everything else is stripped away — health, independence, control, the future you planned — the God who remains is the God you can finally see without distraction.

The Fourth Figure who appeared in the furnace with Shadrach, Meshach, and Abed-nego was only visible inside the fire

(Daniel 3:25). He did not appear before they were thrown in. He did not call to them from outside. He was walking where they walked. Present where the heat was most intense. That has not changed.

The Prophet Who Complained

A different man, a different century, a different kind of suffering — but the same kind of honesty.

Habakkuk opened his book with a complaint.

> *"How long, O LORD, will I call for help, and You will not hear?*
> *I cry out to You, 'Violence!' Yet You do not save.*
> *Why do You make me see iniquity, and cause me to look on wickedness?"*
>
> — Habakkuk 1:2–3

He was watching injustice and demanding to know why God was not intervening. God's answer was not what Habakkuk expected. He was raising up the Babylonians — a nation more wicked than the one Habakkuk was complaining about — to bring judgment (1:5–11). The answer made the question harder, not easier.

But Habakkuk did not walk away. He stood on his guard post and waited (2:1). He took his confusion to God and then he stayed long enough to hear what God would say next. And by the end of the book, without a single one of his circumstances changing, he arrived somewhere extraordinary.

> *"Though the fig tree should not blossom and there be no fruit on
> the vines,*
> *though the yield of the olive should fail and the fields produce no
> food,*
> *though the flock should be cut off from the fold*
> *and there be no cattle in the stalls,*
> *yet I will exult in the LORD,*
> *I will rejoice in the God of my salvation."*
>
> — Habakkuk 3:17–18

"Though... yet." That word *yet* carries the weight of the entire book. Everything on the left side of it is real — the barrenness, the loss, the absence of everything that was supposed to be there. Nothing on that side is denied or minimized. But on the right side of *yet* stands something that does not depend on any of it. Habakkuk's trust was not contingent on his circumstances improving. It was anchored in the character of God — a character he had come to know more deeply precisely because he had been honest enough to bring his hardest questions directly to the source.

—————————

What Belongs to God

Moses, near the end of his life, told Israel something that belongs in this conversation.

> *"The secret things belong to the LORD our God,*
> *but the things revealed belong to us and to our sons forever,*
> *that we may observe all the words of this law."*
>
> — Deuteronomy 29:29

There are two categories. The secret things — the ones God has not disclosed, the purposes He has not explained, the reasons that operate behind the curtain of His sovereignty. And the revealed things — what He has spoken, what He has promised, what He has put in writing and preserved for three thousand years so that a man in a hospital bed and a woman in a chair beside him could read it and know it was true.

Why this man? Why this disease? Why this timeline? These belong to Him. They are among the secret things. And carrying questions that belong to God is a weight no human frame was designed to bear. You were not built for omniscience. You were built for trust.

But what belongs to you is not small.

You know that He is near to the brokenhearted (Psalm 34:18). You know that the valley has an exit — *through,* not *into* (Psalm 23:4). You know that the tent is temporary but you are not (2 Corinthians 5:1). You know that what is sown in weakness will be raised in power, and what is sown a natural body will be raised a spiritual body (1 Corinthians 15:43–44). You know that absent from the body means at home with the Lord (2 Corinthians 5:8). You know that He cannot lie (Titus 1:2). You know that the departure and being with Christ is very much better (Philippians 1:23).

You may not know why. But you know who. And in the silence where the answer to "why" should be, He has placed Himself.

<hr>

A Word to Both of You

Mark — the questions may take a particular shape for you. Why my body? Why this disease and not another? Why couldn't there be more time? Some of these belong among the secret things, and you are free to set them down. You do not have to solve them before you can rest. Job did not solve them. He saw God instead, and said it was enough.

And the question about Bonnie — the one that may surface when you are too tired to push it away — that one has an answer. The third strand holds (Ecclesiastes 4:12). The God who has walked with both of you through this valley will not leave her when you reach the far side. He has never abandoned the brokenhearted. Not once in the entire record of Scripture. He will not begin with her.

Bonnie — your questions have their own weight. Why him? Why not someone else? Why do I have to watch this? And the one that may be hardest of all: why does prayer sometimes feel like it reaches the ceiling and stops?

Psalm 13. David asked "how long" four times in two verses. He did not whisper it. He did not dress it up. He poured it out raw, and God did not turn away. He preserved it — in Scripture, in permanence — so that three thousand years later, a woman sitting beside a hospital bed could open her Bible and find someone who understood the exact shape of her exhaustion.

Your questions are not a failure of faith. They are the sound of a faith that is honest enough to carry the full weight of what it is carrying. Job asked. David asked. Habakkuk asked. God did not turn away from any of them. He will not turn away from you.

There is a kind of rest that does not require answers.

David found it. "I have composed and quieted my soul; like a weaned child rests against his mother, my soul is like a weaned child within me. O Israel, hope in the LORD from this time forth and forever" (Psalm 131:2–3). Not a child still demanding — a child who has settled. Not because every question has been answered, but because the arms holding him are enough.

Job found it. Not in explanation, but in encounter. "I have heard of You by the hearing of the ear; but now my eye sees You" (Job 42:5).

Habakkuk found it. "Though… yet." Everything stripped away on one side. Trust standing firm on the other.

It is not the rest of resolution. It is the rest of trust — the kind that comes when you stop carrying what was never yours to carry and let the secret things belong to the One they have always belonged to. The questions are real. The silence where answers should be is real. And the God who stands in that silence — who did not explain the suffering to Job but showed up inside it, who did not remove the fire from the furnace but walked in it beside three men who trusted Him, who does not promise to make the valley disappear but promises to walk with you through every step of it — He is real too.

You do not have to understand the valley to walk through it. You only have to know the Shepherd.

And you do.

Reflection Questions

1. God rebuked Job's friends who tried to explain the suffering, but honored Job who simply told the truth about his pain. Have you received well-meaning explanations that hurt rather than helped? How did you respond?

2. Job said, "I have heard of You by the hearing of the ear; but now my eye sees You." Has the valley changed your knowledge of God from secondhand to firsthand in any way?

3. Moses distinguished "the secret things" from "the things revealed." What questions are you carrying that might belong in the first category — and what revealed promises can you hold on to instead?

CHAPTER SEVEN

So We Do Not Grieve as Those Who Have No Hope

"But we do not want you to be uninformed, brethren, about those who are asleep, so that you will not grieve as do the rest who have no hope."

— 1 Thessalonians 4:13 (NASB)

You have been holding two things at the same time.

You may not have named them. You may not have realized that the tension you carry is not confusion but coexistence — two realities occupying the same space in your chest, and neither one willing to yield to the other. One of them says this is devastating. The other says this is not the end. One of them keeps you awake at three in the morning. The other is the reason you open your Bible when the morning finally comes. One of them is grief. The other is hope.

And you do not have to choose between them.

That is not a platitude. That is the argument of one of the most carefully constructed passages in the New Testament — a passage written by a man who understood suffering, to a congregation that was buried in it, about a question that was tearing them apart.

Paul wrote to the Thessalonians because they were afraid that their dead were lost. He wrote to tell them they were not. And the way he built his case, line by line, deserves more than a passing glance. It deserves the kind of slow, careful attention that a promise this important has always demanded.

We touched this passage in the first chapter of this book. We read the words "so that you will not grieve as do the rest who have no hope" and noted that Paul did not prohibit grief — he distinguished it. Christian grief is not the world's grief. Not because it hurts less, but because it carries something inside it.

Now it is time to see what it carries.

Why Paul Wrote

The church in Thessalonica was young. Paul had been with them only a short time — Acts 17 tells us it may have been as few as three weeks before opposition forced him to leave. He left behind new believers who were on fire with faith but short on instruction. They believed that Jesus was coming back. They believed it with urgency. And then some of their people began to die.

The question that surfaced was not abstract theology. It was the rawest kind of pastoral crisis: what has happened to our dead? If Jesus is coming back, and they are gone before He arrives, have they missed it? Are they lost? Will we see them again?

Imagine the weight of that question in a room full of people who had just buried a husband, a mother, a child. They were not debating the end times. They were grieving, and their grief was complicated by a fear that the ones they had lost were somehow beyond the reach of the promise.

Paul wrote to end that fear. And he did it not with sentiment but with argument — a sequence of claims, each one resting on the one before it, building toward a conclusion so solid that he could tell them to comfort each other with it.

The Argument

He began with the foundation.

> *"For if we believe that Jesus died and rose again, even so God will bring*
> *with Him those who have fallen asleep in Jesus."*
> — 1 Thessalonians 4:14

The word *if* here is not expressing doubt. In the Greek, Paul used a first-class conditional — *ei* with the indicative — which assumes the condition is true. A clearer rendering of his meaning would be: "Since we believe that Jesus died and rose again." Paul was not questioning the resurrection. He was building on it. The resurrection of Christ is not merely an article of faith to be affirmed. It is the load-bearing wall of the entire structure. Everything that follows in this passage depends on it being true.

And what follows is staggering in its directness: "even so God will bring with Him those who have fallen asleep in Jesus." The logic is plain. Jesus died. Jesus rose. Therefore, those who belong to Him and have died will be brought with Him when He comes. The fate of the believer is bound to the fate of Christ. What happened to Him will happen to them. His resurrection is not merely the proof that resurrection is possible. It is the guarantee that it will happen.

Paul went further. He wanted them to know that he was not offering his own opinion.

> *"For this we say to you by the word of the Lord, that we who are alive*
> *and remain until the coming of the Lord, will not precede*
> *those who have fallen asleep."*
>
> — 1 Thessalonians 4:15

"By the word of the Lord." This was not Paul speculating. This was not Paul offering pastoral comfort drawn from his own experience. This was revelation. What he was about to tell them carried the authority of Christ Himself. And the first thing he said with that authority was designed to address their specific fear: those who are alive when the Lord returns will not have any advantage over those who have already died. The dead are not behind. They are not left out. If anything, Paul said, they go first.

> *"For the Lord Himself will descend from heaven with a shout,*
> *with the voice of the archangel and with the trumpet of God,*
> *and the dead in Christ will rise first."*
>
> — 1 Thessalonians 4:16

The dead in Christ will rise first. Before anything else happens, before the living are gathered, the dead are raised. The Thessalonians were afraid their loved ones would miss the Lord's return. Paul told them they would lead it.

And then the reunion.

"Then we who are alive and remain will be caught up together with them
in the clouds to meet the Lord in the air, and so we shall always be with the Lord."

— 1 Thessalonians 4:17

Three words in that verse change everything, and they are easy to rush past if you are reading quickly. The first is *together*. Not separately. Not in different places or at different times. Together — the living and the raised, reunited. The separation that the valley is creating has an end. The distance that death imposes is not permanent.

The second word is *always*. "So we shall always be with the Lord." Not for a season. Not until the next catastrophe. Always. The reunion that begins at that moment does not end. The separation has an expiration date. The togetherness does not.

The third word is actually the first word of the verse: *then*. It is a word of sequence. First the dead rise. Then the living are gathered. Then — together — always with the Lord. Paul was not painting a vague picture of "a better place." He was laying out an order of events with the precision of someone who had received it directly from the Lord and wanted no part of it to be misunderstood.

––––––––––––

What Hope Means

The word *hope* in English has become soft. We use it for things we wish for but cannot count on. "I hope it doesn't rain." "I hope I get the job." It carries the flavor of uncertainty — a desire with no guarantee attached.

That is not what the New Testament means by hope.

The Greek word is *elpis*, and in the New Testament it does not describe a wish. It describes a confident expectation based on what God has said and done. It is forward-looking certainty, not backward-looking nostalgia. When Paul said the Thessalonians should not grieve as those who have "no hope," he was not telling them to feel optimistic. He was telling them that they possessed something the rest of the world did not: a promise backed by a resurrection.

The distinction matters because hope, in the biblical sense, is not a feeling. Feelings rise and fall. You know this. There are mornings when the hope feels close enough to touch and nights when it feels like a word you heard once in a sermon that has nothing to do with the beeping monitors and the exhaustion and the fear. But hope does not depend on your ability to feel it at any given moment. It depends on the faithfulness of the One who made the promise.

Paul made this connection explicit in 1 Corinthians 15, where he built the most sustained argument for the resurrection in the entire New Testament. And in the middle of it, he used a word that ties the future to the past with an unbreakable cord.

> *"But now Christ has been raised from the dead,*
> *the first fruits of those who are asleep."*
> — 1 Corinthians 15:20

First fruits. In the agricultural world Paul's readers knew, the first fruits were not the entire harvest. They were the initial portion —

the part that came up first and guaranteed that the rest was coming. When the first sheaf of grain appeared, the farmer did not wonder whether there would be more. The first fruits were the proof and the promise of the full harvest to come.

Christ is the first fruits of the dead. His resurrection is not an isolated event. It is the first sheaf. And if the first sheaf has come up out of the ground, the harvest is certain. What happened to Him on the third day outside Jerusalem will happen to everyone who belongs to Him. The tomb is not the end of the story. It is the place where the seed goes into the ground — and as we saw in an earlier chapter, what goes into the ground does not look like what comes up.

> *"It is sown a perishable body, it is raised an imperishable body;*
> *it is sown in dishonor, it is raised in glory;*
> *it is sown in weakness, it is raised in power;*
> *it is sown a natural body, it is raised a spiritual body."*
> — 1 Corinthians 15:42–44

The body that fails — the one that cancer has been dismantling piece by piece — is the seed, not the tree. And seeds, by their nature, do not look like what they become. An acorn bears no resemblance to an oak. A dry, buried kernel of wheat looks nothing like the green stalk that breaks through the soil. What is sown in weakness will be raised in power. What is sown perishable will be raised imperishable. The failing body is not the final form. It is the planting.

The Time Between

There is a question that surfaces in the quiet hours, and honesty requires that we address it: what happens between death and that resurrection day? What is the experience of the one who has departed? Is there a gap? Is there waiting? Is there awareness?

Scripture speaks to this, but it speaks with a brevity that should make us careful. What has been revealed is clear. What has not been revealed is not ours to fill in with speculation.

Paul told the Corinthians that to be absent from the body is to be at home with the Lord (2 Corinthians 5:8). He told the Philippians that to depart and be with Christ was "very much better" (Philippians 1:23) — *pollō mallon kreisson*, stacked comparatives in the Greek, as if a single word for "better" was not strong enough to carry the reality. Jesus told the thief on the cross, "Today you shall be with Me in Paradise" (Luke 23:43). Today. Not eventually. Not after a period of waiting. Today.

These three passages, taken together, point in the same direction: the believer who dies is with Christ, and that transition is immediate rather than delayed. The details of what that experience is like — what is seen, what is felt, what the awareness consists of — Scripture does not elaborate. And where Scripture is quiet, this book will be quiet too. We do not need to know the mechanics of the crossing to trust the One who meets us on the other side. Chapter 5 of this book walked through what Scripture reveals about what is there: Christ is there, rest is there, wholeness is there, recognition is there. That is what the text gives us. It is enough.

What the text does not give us is reason to fear the transition. Paul did not speak of it with dread. He spoke of it with longing —

"having the desire to depart and be with Christ, for that is very much better" (Philippians 1:23). He used the word *courage* twice in the span of three verses when describing the prospect of leaving the body (2 Corinthians 5:6, 8). Whatever the crossing looks like, the Man who walked through it first — who tasted death for everyone (Hebrews 2:9) and then broke it open from the inside — has gone ahead to prepare a place (John 14:2). The path is not uncharted. It has been walked by the Shepherd Himself.

Grief and Hope, Side by Side

So where does this leave you — right now, today, in the middle of the valley?

It leaves you in the place Paul described: grieving, but not as those who have no hope. Holding both. Setting neither one down. The grief is real because the love is real, and love does not let go of what it is losing without pain. If it did, it would not be love. The hope is real because the resurrection is real, and the resurrection does not become less true on the nights when you are too exhausted to feel it.

They walk together. They have always walked together. Martha stood at the road outside Bethany and said to Jesus, "Lord, if You had been here, my brother would not have died" — that was grief, raw and unfiltered. And in the very next breath: "Even now I know that whatever You ask of God, God will give You" (John 11:21–22). Grief and hope, in the same woman, in the same sentence, separated by a single breath. Jesus did not tell her to choose one. He gave her a reason to hold both: "I am the resurrection and the life; he who believes in Me will live even if he dies" (John 11:25).

He did not say "I know about the resurrection" or "I will arrange the resurrection." He said "I *am* the resurrection." The hope is not an event on a calendar. It is a Person. And that Person has been walking with you through every chapter of this valley — the companion in the shadow, the fourth figure in the fire, the one who wept real tears at a real tomb and then called the dead man out of it by name.

Comfort One Another

Paul closed this passage with a sentence that is easy to overlook but that carries the weight of everything before it.

> *"Therefore comfort one another with these words."*
> — 1 Thessalonians 4:18

He did not say "comfort one another with your feelings about these words." He did not say "comfort one another with your own insights and experiences." He said "with these words." The words themselves — the specific claims about Christ's return, about the dead rising first, about the reunion, about the *always* — these are the comfort. They were written to be spoken aloud to people who are hurting. They were designed for hospital rooms and living rooms and gravesides and all the quiet, devastating places where grief does its work.

This passage was not written for theologians. It was written for the Thessalonians — ordinary believers who had buried people they loved and were afraid those people were lost. Paul gave them words, and told them to give those words to each other.

That is what this chapter is doing. It is handing you the words Paul handed them. Not because words on a page can take the pain away — they cannot — but because these particular words carry a promise that outlasts the pain. The separation is temporary. The reunion is permanent. The dead in Christ rise first. Together. Always. These are not wishes. They are the revealed will of God, spoken by the authority of Christ, confirmed by a resurrection that has already happened, and preserved in Scripture for exactly this moment — when you need them most and trust them least.

--- --- --- ---

A Word to Both of You

Mark — the promise in this passage is yours. The body that is failing you is the seed, not the tree. What is sown in weakness will be raised in power. And the crossing, whenever it comes, is not a departure into the unknown. It is an arrival. Paul called it home. Jesus called it Paradise. And He said *today* — not eventually, not after a long silence, but today. The Shepherd who has walked with you through every mile of this valley will walk with you through that last step too. He has been through it Himself. He knows the way.

Bonnie — the promise in this passage is also yours, and Paul wrote it with you in mind. He wrote it for people who were left behind and afraid. He wrote it so that your grief would not have to carry the weight of despair on top of everything else it is already carrying. The separation is real. The empty chair will be real. The silence in the house will be real. But the *always* is real too. "So we shall always be with the Lord." The timing is different for each of you, but the destination is the same. And between now and then, you are not walking alone. The third strand holds. The rod and the staff have not been set down. The God who is near to the brokenhearted will be near to you — not eventually, not in theory, but in the specific, daily, three-in-the-morning reality of learning to live in a world that has changed.

The valley is not over. There is still one chapter left to walk. But you are not where you started. You have walked through the shadow and found that it could not harm you, because a shadow is not the thing itself. You have walked through the silence and found that silence was not absence. You have walked through the failing of the body and found that you are not the tent. You have walked through the exhaustion and found that walking and not fainting is the eagle's promise dressed in ordinary clothes. You have walked through the unanswered questions and found that the God who did not explain Himself to Job showed up inside the furnace instead.

And now you have walked into the heart of the promise: that what is happening is not the end. That the dead in Christ will rise. That the living and the raised will be together. That *always* means always.

There is one more step. The valley has an exit.

We are almost through.

Reflection Questions

1. Paul said the dead in Christ will rise first and that we will be together, always, with the Lord. Which of those three words — rise, together, always — speaks most directly to your fear right now?

2. Hope in the New Testament is not a wish but a confident expectation based on what God has done. On the hardest nights, what is the difference between wishing and hoping — and how do you hold on to the second?

3. Paul told the Thessalonians to "comfort one another with these words." Who in your life needs to hear these specific promises — and is there someone who could speak them back to you?

CHAPTER EIGHT

I Will Fear No Evil

"Even though I walk through the valley of the shadow
of death,
I fear no evil, for You are with me."
— Psalm 23:4 (NASB)

We began here.

Seven chapters ago, you opened this book — perhaps in a hospital room, perhaps in a house that has grown too quiet, perhaps in a chair beside a bed where someone you love is sleeping the restless sleep of a body that is very tired. You opened it carrying the full weight of the valley, and the first thing you read was this: you didn't choose this.

That is still true. Nothing in these pages has changed what is happening. The diagnosis has not reversed. The treatments have not suddenly started working again. The valley is still the valley, and the shadow is still the shadow, and the long, slow ache of watching someone you love walk toward the end of their life on this earth — or of being the one who is walking — has not lifted because you read a book.

But you are not where you started.

You have walked through seven chapters of the valley with the Shepherd, and even if you cannot see it clearly yet, the ground beneath your feet has been changing. The entrance to the valley is behind you. You have been moving through it — not around it, not over it, but *through* it, the way David said you would. And the same psalm that opened this book has one more thing to say before it is finished.

--- --- --- ---

The Table

David did something extraordinary in the fifth verse of the twenty-third Psalm. Without transition, without explanation, the imagery shifted. For four verses, he had been walking through a valley with a shepherd. And then, suddenly:

> *"You prepare a table before me in the presence of my enemies;*
> *You have anointed my head with oil;*
> *My cup overflows."*
> — Psalm 23:5

A table. In the valley. In the presence of enemies. Not after the enemies are defeated. Not once the valley is behind him. Right here. Right now. In the middle of everything that is still threatening, still pressing, still dark — God prepares a table.

This is not a picture of escape. It is a picture of provision in the midst of what has not yet ended. The enemies are still present. The valley may not yet be behind you. The shadow has not fully lifted. And God sets a table.

What does that look like in a hospital room? It looks like the conversation you did not expect to have — the one where laughter came from somewhere and surprised you both. It looks like the friend who showed up with food and stayed long enough to sit but not so long that it became exhausting. It looks like the morning you opened your Bible out of habit more than hunger and a verse you have read a hundred times said something you had never heard before. It looks like the nurse who treated him with dignity when dignity felt like the last thing left. It looks like the prayer that finally broke through the ceiling — not because the answer changed, but because the Presence became undeniable.

The table is not the end of the valley. It is grace inside the valley. It is God saying, "You are still here, and so am I, and before we take the next step, sit down. Eat. Let Me show you that I have not forgotten you."

David said his cup overflowed. Not merely filled — overflowed. There is a kind of abundance that has nothing to do with circumstances and everything to do with the character of the One who is providing. You have seen that abundance, even here. You may not have called it that. You may have called it "a good day" or "a better night" or "he seemed like himself for a few hours." But those moments were not accidents. They were the table. They were the oil on your head. They were the cup running over in the presence of enemies that have not yet left the room.

What Follows

And then David said the most audacious thing in the entire psalm.

Surely. Not hopefully. Not possibly. Not if things go well. Surely. David looked back over the valley — the shadow, the fear, the rod and the staff, the table in the presence of enemies — and his conclusion was not "I survived." His conclusion was that goodness and lovingkindness had been following him the entire time.

The Hebrew word translated "follow" is *yirdephuni*, from *radaph*. It does not mean to walk quietly behind. It means to pursue. To chase. It is the same word used for pursuing an enemy in battle, for hunting, for chasing something down with determination and intent. David said that goodness and lovingkindness were not merely accompanying him through life. They were chasing him. Running him down. Pursuing him with a relentlessness that matched the relentlessness of the valley itself.

You may not feel pursued by goodness right now. The valley has a way of narrowing your vision until all you can see is the next step, the next appointment, the next difficult conversation. But David's testimony was not based on what he could see in the moment. It was based on what he knew about the Shepherd — the same Shepherd who had walked with him through the shadow, who had armed Himself with a rod and a staff, who had prepared a table before the enemies were gone, who had never once left his side.

Goodness and lovingkindness have been following you too. Through every chapter of this valley. Through the diagnosis and the treatments and the hospital stays. Through the three-in-the-morning fear and the silence that felt like abandonment. Through the days when your body would not do what you told it and the days when caregiving took everything you had and asked for more. Through the unanswered questions and the well-meaning friends who tried to answer them anyway. Through all of it — not in front of you where you could see them clearly, but behind you, where pursuing things run, where you can only see them when you stop and look back.

And then the final line. The destination.

"I will dwell in the house of the LORD forever."

Not visit. Dwell. The Hebrew is *v'shavti* — and I will return, and I will remain. It carries the sense of coming home to a place you belong and never leaving again. This is not a temporary stay. This is not another tent. This is the building from God — eternal, in the heavens, not made with hands (2 Corinthians 5:1). The dwelling place Jesus spoke of in the upper room the night before He died: "In My Father's house are many dwelling places; if it were not so, I would have told you; for I go to prepare a place for you" (John 14:2).

Forever. The word that answers the valley. The valley is temporary. Forever is not. The shadow passes. The dwelling remains. The separation that the valley imposes — between husband and wife, between the living and the dead, between the way things were and the way things are — that separation has an expiration date. But the dwelling in the house of the Lord does not.

For the One Who Goes First

Mark — this chapter, and this book, has been walking toward something, and it is time to say it plainly.

You are not walking toward an ending. You are walking toward a beginning.

The body that has carried you through every year of your life is failing. You know this better than anyone, because you are the one living inside it, and you feel the difference between what you could do a year ago and what you can do today. That loss is real and it is grievous and no one should minimize it by rushing past it to get to the hope. Your body has served you faithfully, and the slow betrayal of it is one of the heaviest things a person can carry.

But you are not the tent (2 Corinthians 5:1). You have never been the tent. The tent is what you live in, not what you are. And when the canvas finally gives way — when the perishable puts on the imperishable and the mortal puts on immortality (1 Corinthians 15:53–54) — what is waiting is not another tent. It is a building from God, eternal in the heavens. What is sown in weakness will be raised in power. What goes into the ground as a seed will come up as something that bears no resemblance to what was planted, the way an oak bears no resemblance to the acorn it grew from.

The crossing itself — the step between here and there — is the one part of the journey Scripture does not describe in detail. And that silence used to trouble me until I realized what fills it. Jesus said, "Today you shall be with Me in Paradise" (Luke 23:43). Paul said that to depart and be with Christ is very much better (Philippians 1:23). To be absent from the body is to be at home with the Lord (2 Corinthians 5:8). The details of the crossing are not revealed, but the One who meets you on the far side is fully revealed. He is the same Shepherd who has been walking with you through every step of this valley. The same one whose rod and staff have been protecting and guiding you. The same one who prepared a table for you in the presence of enemies. He does not hand you off to someone else at the threshold. He is already there. He has been through it Himself. He knows the way, because He is the way (John 14:6).

And the first thing that will be gone — the very first thing — is the pain. "He will wipe away every tear from their eyes; and there will no longer be any death; there will no longer be any mourning, or crying, or pain; the first things have passed away" (Revelation 21:4). Not reduced. Not managed. Gone. And notice the intimacy of that promise: *He* will wipe away every tear. Personally. The God of the universe, who holds the sea in its boundaries and calls the stars by name, will wipe the tears from your face the way a father wipes the tears from his child's.

You will fear no evil. Not because evil is not real, but because the shadow cannot harm you. It never could. A shadow requires a light source behind it, and the light behind this shadow is brighter than anything the valley has shown you.

For the One Who Remains

Bonnie — when that day comes, the house will be very quiet.

There is no way around that sentence, and this book has promised from the beginning not to walk around things but through them. The chair beside the bed will be empty. The routines that have structured your days — the medications, the appointments, the conversations with nurses, the drive to the hospital and the drive home — will stop. And in the space where all of that was, there will be silence. And in the silence, the grief will come in waves that no one who has not stood in that exact place can fully understand.

You will not grieve as one who has no hope (1 Thessalonians 4:13). But you will grieve. And the grieving will not be brief, because the love was not small. Jacob mourned many days (Genesis 37:34). David composed a lament and ordered it taught to the people (2 Samuel 1:17–18). Jesus wept at the tomb of a man He was about to raise from the dead (John 11:35). The God who made you to love deeply does not expect you to lose deeply without feeling the full weight of it. Your tears are not a failure of faith. They are the proof of what he meant to you, and that proof honors both the man and the God who made him.

But you will not be alone.

The third strand holds (Ecclesiastes 4:12). It held before the valley, it has held through the valley, and it will hold after the valley. The cord of three strands does not unravel when one strand is taken, because the third strand was always the strongest. He will be with you in the first morning and the second morning and the hundredth morning. He will be with you when the well-meaning people have gone back to their own lives and the cards have stopped coming and the world has moved on in the way the world always does. He will be with you at three in the morning when the house is dark and the absence is loudest. The LORD is near to the brokenhearted and saves those who are crushed in spirit (Psalm 34:18). *Qarov* — right beside you. In the chair beside the bed. In the car on the way home. In the kitchen on the first morning when the coffee is for one.

And there is a promise that belongs to you as specifically as the resurrection promise belongs to him. Isaiah said it, and it has not expired:

> *"Yet those who wait for the LORD will gain new strength;*
> *they will mount up with wings like eagles,*
> *they will run and not get tired,*
> *they will walk and not become weary."*
>
> — Isaiah 40:31

You may never feel like an eagle again. You may not run. But if you walk and do not grow weary — if you get up tomorrow and the day after that and the day after that, and you keep putting one foot in front of the other in a world that has fundamentally changed — that is the eagle's promise dressed in ordinary clothes. That is not failure. That is the quietest and most persistent form of victory that faith produces. And it is enough.

Through

The word that has carried this book from the first page to the last is the smallest word in the psalm: *through*.

Even though I walk *through* the valley of the shadow of death.

Through means there is another side. The valley is not a destination. It is a passage. It has an entrance, and it has an exit. For one of you, the exit leads to the house of the Lord — the dwelling place, the building not made with hands, the place where every tear is wiped away and pain is not reduced but gone. For the other, the exit leads to a different kind of life on this side of eternity — a life marked by the valley, changed by it permanently, but not defined by it. Because the same psalm that describes the valley also describes what is on the other side: goodness and lovingkindness, pursuing you with a relentlessness you did not ask for and cannot outrun.

Both exits lead to the same home. The timing is different. The path is different. But the Shepherd is the same, and the destination is the same, and the *forever* in the last line of the psalm is the same forever for both of you.

> *"And I will dwell in the house of the LORD forever."*
> — Psalm 23:6

You have walked through the valley of the shadow of death.

You have walked through the silence and found that silence was not absence — that the God who seemed far away was closer than the breath in your lungs, closer than the hand holding yours across the hospital bed. You have walked through the failing of the body and found that you are not the tent, that the canvas is temporary but what it carries is eternal. You have walked through the exhaustion and the anticipatory grief and the guilt that had no right to be there, and you have walked and not fainted, and that is the eagle's promise, and it was always enough. You have walked through the unanswered questions and found that the God who did not explain Himself to Job stepped into the furnace instead, and that His presence was the answer to the question behind all the other questions. You have walked through the intersection of grief and hope and found that they are not enemies — that you can hold the devastation in one hand and the promise in the other and neither one cancels the other out.

And you have arrived here — not at the end of the pain, not with every question answered, not with a theology that makes the valley make sense. But with a Shepherd. The same one who was with you at the entrance is with you now. The rod and the staff have not been set down. The table has been prepared. The cup has overflowed. Goodness and lovingkindness have been chasing you the whole way, even when you could not see them, even when the shadow was so dark that you could not see anything at all.

The valley is real. The shadow is real. The grief is real.

And so is He.

And that is enough.

Reflection Questions

1. David said goodness and lovingkindness were pursuing him through the valley. When you stop and look back over these weeks and months, where can you see them — even if they were hidden at the time?

2. The table was prepared "in the presence of enemies" — not after the valley was over. What has the table looked like for you in the middle of this season?

3. "Through" means the valley has an exit. Whether that exit is the house of the Lord or a changed life on this side of eternity — what does it look like, today, to trust the word "through"?

Scripture Index

1 Corinthians

2 Corinthians

Ephesians

Philippians

1 Thessalonians

Titus

Hebrews

1 Peter

Revelation